Secrets of the kitchen

Secrets of the kitchen

FRANÇOISE DUBARRY

MONIQUE DUVEAU

FRANÇOIS GOUDIER

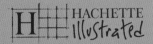
HACHETTE
Illustrated

CONTENTS

Sauces, marinades & dressings 8

Herbs, seasonings, spices & condiments 20

Fresh vegetables, pulses & mushrooms 40

Fish, shellfish & seafood 62

Meat, poultry & game 76

Eggs & dairy products 90

Pasta, rice & cereals 100

Fresh & dried fruits, conserves & jams 112

Bread, pastries & desserts 130

Beverages, alcohol & infusions 146

Supplements 154

FOREWORD

COPIED, CUT OUT AND DISCOLOURED RECIPES CLUTTERING UP OUR SHELVES; recipes with notes scribbled on them; recipes that somehow didn't quite turn out right; recipes that needed a little expert tweaking to produce the perfect dish. We've all come across recipes where, despite following the instructions to the letter, something simply doesn't quite add up: the mayonnaise curdles, the apples are too hard, the cake sticks to the sides of the baking tin, the cream is annoyingly lumpy...

Let's hark back to the cooks of yesteryear, as well as taking a few tips from modern day chefs; let's explore those secrets of the kitchen without which we couldn't pull off the flawless recipe or indeed perfect our culinary knowledge. My grandmother used to reveal her tricks of the trade in veiled terms, through gestures: she possessed the know-how derived from experience. 'The melon isn't ripe!' – 'How do you know?' I would ask. 'It's obvious, you can sense it.' And what about egg custard?' 'You can't take your eyes off it for a second!' Such culinary skills are like rites of passage, tools that are handed down from one generation to the next. These nuggets of wisdom result in softer tarts, more tender meat, more flavoursome sauces ...

This book is not designed to be stored in a library, but rather to be kept at hand, on the kitchen table, to be used as a daily reference. It contains a wealth of information that is accessible to all those who are determined to master the art of cooking and gain a fine reputation as a cook. Some secrets that concern us are all about the magic and mystery surrounding certain items; universal secrets that are also endowed with great poetry.

SAUCES, MARINADES & DRESSINGS

IT IS THE SAUCE OR THE DRESSING THAT BRINGS OUT THE BEST IN A DISH, ITS RICHNESS AND ITS FLAVOUR WHICH MAKES IT STAND OUT FROM OTHER DISHES AND GIVES IT THAT SOMETHING EXTRA. THERE IS AN OLD SAYING, 'A GOOD SAUCE MAKES EVERY MOUTHFUL GO DOWN BETTER', BUT SUCCESS SOMETIMES ALSO REQUIRES A DASH OF MAGIC. COOKERY EXPERT, HERVÉ THYS, EMPHASISES, 'THE TRUE ART OF COOKING LIES NOT IN DELIVERING THE PERFECT SOUFFLÉ EACH TIME, BUT IN ANTICIPATING THAT PASTIS WOULD GO RATHER WELL WITH VEAL ESCALOPE.'

SAUCES

The right utensils

Make sure you that you have the right utensils for making sauces. A whisk is essential for blending, and a fine sieve or a muslin cloth is useful for straining liquids.

- If you need to set aside or reheat a sauce, place it in a bain-marie, over a very low heat, stirring at intervals with a whisk.
- If a sauce is a bit bland, pep it up with a drop of lemon juice or vinegar.
- If a sauce is too salty, two pieces of raw potato, added while cooking, will absorb the excess salt. If a sauce is too peppery, all you need to do is add a drop of milk or crème fraîche.
- To thicken a runny sauce mix a teaspoon of potato starch or cornflour in a small amount of the liquid, add to the sauce, and cook for a few minutes longer.
- If the sauce has separated, with greasy blobs on the surface, add a little water and repeat the cooking process.
- To skim a sauce, tilt the container and draw off the surplus fat using a skimmer or a tablespoon.
- Skimmed meat juices add a wonderful flavour to salads. You can also freeze the skimmed juices in an ice cube tray; the frozen cubes will come in handy for adding substance to wine-based sauces or enhancing the flavour of onion soup.
- To make gravy from the juices of roast meat, pour a glass of boiling water into the roasting pan, stir with a spatula and reduce over a high heat. You could substitute lemon juice, spirits, wine, or crème fraîche for deglazing meat juices. Strain the gravy before serving.
- Tip: deglaze the juices from veal escalope with a little white wine and a dash of pastis!

STOCK: follow the example of top chefs and make your own stock as a sauce base for veal, poultry and smoked fish dishes. The secret is to create a multi-purpose stock and keep it in the freezer or store it in the fridge in small, sterilised jars.
- When preparing stock, avoid crushing meat on the bone or the vegetables; instead press down gently with the back of a ladle: the resulting liquid will be much clearer.

No more lumps

Avoid lumps forming in your béchamel sauce by gradually adding warm milk to the melted butter and flour, away from the heat and stirring until the ingredients form a smooth paste. Beat with a whisk, return to the heat and cook, stirring continually, until the sauce has thickened to the required consistency. If any lumps remain, strain the sauce through a sieve.

■ Poultry stock cubes can be substituted when making a poultry-based sauce, or to enhance a bland-tasting veal sauce.

MAYONNAISE: for best results, all the ingredients need to be at room temperature (remove the eggs from the refrigerator at least three hours beforehand).

■ As soon as the mayonnaise begins to form, add a drop of vinegar or lemon juice for smoother results. If the mayonnaise is too runny, add a tablespoon of boiling vinegar and continue whisking.

■ If mayonnaise separates, you can save it by placing a tablespoon of Dijon mustard in a separate bowl and gradually incorporating the curdled mayonnaise, whisking continuously, until the mixture has regained its correct consistency.

■ Season the mayonnaise according to the dish it is meant to accompany by adding flavours such as curry powder, chopped chives, saffron or tomato purée.

■ To prepare a lighter version of mayonnaise without using eggs, simply blend a little olive oil with some Dijon mustard, whisking continuously.

■ Don't throw away the unused egg whites when making mayonnaise. Whisk them until stiff and then gently fold into the mayonnaise. This is especially enjoyable with asparagus.

GARLIC MAYONNAISE: for a milder tasting garlic mayonnaise, use steam-cooked garlic instead of raw garlic.

BÉCHAMEL SAUCE: allow 1 pint/½ litre of milk per heaped tablespoon of flour and ½ oz/15 g of butter.

■ The sauce will be of a lighter consistency if you use cornflour instead of flour.

■ If your béchamel is too thick, add a drop of milk to the mixture, if it's too salty, add a little crème fraîche.

■ For a richer béchamel, add two egg yolks, thinned in little cream, just before the sauce has finished cooking.

■ Flavour a béchamel sauce with grated nutmeg, a pinch of mixed spice (a blend of cinnamon, nutmeg, cloves and ground ginger – see page 35), or a pinch of ground white pepper and coriander seeds.

■ Vegetables should be well drained before coating with béchamel sauce, otherwise the water they produce during cooking will make the sauce too runny.

Garlic mayonnaise

To produce a really smooth garlic mayonnaise, add a small peeled, boiled potato to the mixture.

Classic mayonnaise

As there can be no substitute for homemade mayonnaise, here is the recipe for classic mayonnaise, which you can season to taste.

Serves 4:
■ 1 egg yolk
■ 1 tablespoon Dijon mustard
■ pinch of salt
■ 1 twist of the pepper mill
■ ⅓ pt/20 cl oil
■ 1 teaspoon lemon juice or wine vinegar

Whisk together the egg yolk, mustard, salt and pepper, then trickle the oil in slowly, particularly at the start, whipping continuously. As it starts to thicken add the lemon juice or vinegar, then continue adding the oil while still beating.

■ Brighten up a bland vegetable dish by covering it with a highly spiced béchamel sauce flavoured with tomato purée. The result is amazing and exceedingly tasty.

WINE-BASED SAUCES: will be milder if you flambé the wine first to reduce its acidity; this applies to both red and white wine. After cooking add two semi-dried Agen prunes.

■ Add colour to stews and brown sauces by adding two squares of plain chocolate or a heaped teaspoon of bitter cocoa powder. The mild chocolate taste will add a finishing touch to the flavour of the sauce.

■ Freeze any leftover wine-based sauce in a small freezer container; it will come in handy for enhancing steak tournedos or pasta dishes.

THE EGG LIAISON: eggs are used to thicken and lend a creamy consistency to sauces, especially white sauces. In a small bowl, mix a beaten egg yolk and a tablespoon of vinegar with some of the sauce. Return the mixture to the rest of the sauce, stir vigorously and cook for a few minutes over a gentle heat.

■ Add egg white to the water when cooking blanquette of veal, pork tongue or garlic soup; it helps clarify and add bulk to stocks or sauces.

TOMATO SAUCE: autumn often sees the arrival of a glut of outdoor-grown tomatoes in fresh produce markets so now's the time to stock up on tomatoes for the winter! In the past, people used to preserve tomato sauce by adding salicylic acid to chopped tomatoes, to halt fermentation. The mixture would then be stored in glass jars, topped with oil to prevent deterioration, and sealed. Bottling and preserving fruit and vegetables was commonplace from one season to the next.

■ If tomatoes have not ripened fully, reduce their acidity by adding a teaspoon of sugar, a few drops of balsamic vinegar and a pinch of bicarbonate of soda.

■ A time-saving tip is to bulk freeze home-made tomato sauce in small, individual containers, then all you have to do is reheat individual portions.

■ Improve canned tomato purée by adding a bouquet garni, a little chopped onion and a few slices of garlic. Purée can also be blended with meat stock.

Ravigote sauce

This classic French sauce accompanies meat stews and steamed vegetables and it can also be used to add flavour to leftover ingredients. Make sure that you add enough gherkins and capers to bring out the full flavour.

Serves 6:
■ 2 hard-boiled eggs
■ 1 tablespoon mustard
■ 2 tablespoons sherry vinegar
■ 3 tablespoons olive oil
■ pinch of salt and pepper
■ 1 sprig parsley finely chopped
■ 1 shallot peeled and chopped
■ 1 tablespoon capers
■ 1 tablespoon chopped gherkins

Crush the hard-boiled eggs with a fork and put through a sieve. Add the mustard, sherry vinegar, olive oil and a pinch of salt and pepper. Prepare using the method for mayonnaise; finally add the parsley, shallot, capers and gherkins.

Quick tomato sauce

To make a quick tomato sauce, cut the tomatoes into quarters, leaving their skins on, and mix in a blender. If you only need to prepare one or two tomatoes, grate them roughly to extract the pulp, discarding the skins. For both methods, cook the tomato pulp with some thinly sliced garlic, in very hot olive oil, over a high heat. The sauce turns slightly yellow while cooking. Reduce the sauce to the desired consistency, neither too liquid nor too thick. Add a pinch of saffron to bring out the flavour.

DRESSINGS

VINAIGRETTE DRESSING: this dressing seems quite straightforward and yet it is often a flop! Frequently it is as a result of too much vinegar or too much mustard! Use no more than one tablespoon of vinegar to every three tablespoons of oil; adding a teaspoon of French mustard to the mixture can rectify excess vinegar.

■ Salt does not dissolve in oil, so it has to be dissolved in the vinegar first before adding to the oil.

■ If you find that the vinegar you are using is too sharp, add a drop of soy sauce.

■ Or try using balsamic vinegar, which is the least acidic vinegar available.

■ Chopped shallots and a pinch of curry powder added to vinaigrette goes very well with salad.

■ To save time, prepare vinaigrette dressing in advance and store it in a small bottle or in a hermetically sealed jar. Shake the bottle or jar each time, before use.

VEGETABLE OILS: should be stored away from the light, preferably in a dark-coloured bottle, to prevent them from turning rancid.

■ Walnut oil goes well with cider vinegar; use them in a dressing for a mixed green salad of young leaves and shoots with pickled gizzards.

■ Sesame oil adds flavour to green salads, grated carrots and other crudités.

VINEGAR: don't panic if you haven't got any vinegar to hand, because a glass of wine, brought to the boil and reduced by a quarter to the point where the liquid begins to thicken, will do instead. Mask any acidity with a pinch of sugar.

■ Flavour your own vinegar with white wine or add a few sprigs of rosemary, thyme or basil to the bottle. Other flavours you can add include elderflower, or five or six cloves of garlic. Bring the vinegar to the boil in a small pan and pour it into the jar, seal and leave to steep for 15 days before use.

■ Cider vinegar goes well with honey. Add two tablespoons of honey to every 1½ pint/1 litre of vinegar and leave to steep for several weeks. Use it for seasoning stewed apple compote and for deglazing fried foie gras.

■ Add a few drops of vinegar to cooking oil before frying; foods fried in this way absorb less fat.

Flavoured oil

You can flavour your own olive oil in various ways. To make lemon flavoured oil for cooking fish add three lemon slices plus the grated rind of a lemon to the bottle. Add a sprig of rosemary, oregano and a large stalk of basil to the bottle to make a herb flavoured oil for salads. Oil flavoured with two sticks of cinnamon and four cloves is used for confectionery. All flavoured oil combinations should be left to steep for 15 days before use.

Mona dressing

This is a dressing that you can make throughout the summer months, using readily available seasonal herbs to add fresh flavours to vegetables, salads and fish.

Serves 4:
■ 2 sprigs flat-leaved parsley
■ 1 sprig tarragon
■ 2 pinches lemon rind grated
■ 1 clove garlic grated
■ 1 shallot grated
■ 1 teaspoon tomato paste or purée
■ 4 tablespoons olive oil

Finely chop the herbs and add the grated lemon rind, garlic and shallot and the tomato paste or purée. Blend all the ingredients together with the olive oil. Stored in a hermetically sealed jar, this dressing will keep in the refrigerator, all summer long. Replenish every week.

■ If a white tablecloth is stained with vinegar, rub it with a solution of one part bleach to ten parts water, then rinse carefully in cold water.

MARINADES

■ Marinades can be used to tenderise meat and fish and to add flavour to ingredients. Keep the marinade in the refrigerator or in a cool place.

■ For a quick marinade where the meat or fish doesn't need to be marinated for any length of time, use a marinade of herb-flavoured oil, with a little lemon juice and vinegar. This is ideal for grilled meats, or raw meat or fish recipes.

■ Take care when using lemon because it blanches and cooks the flesh. In a recipe for raw fish carpaccio, add the lemon juice at the last minute.

■ Meat needs to marinate for between 12 and 24 hours in a wine-based marinade. Don't forget the vinegar, because it is this ingredient that tenderises the meat. Two tablespoons of oil are also important because they help reduce the acidity of the wine and prevent oxidisation. Make sure that the pieces of meat or fish are completely covered by the liquid; also take care to drain off all the liquid and pat the meat or fish dry before cooking.

■ If you don't have 12 hours to spare before cooking the meat, boil the wine marinade for 30 minutes, chill immediately, then immerse the pieces of meat in the marinade. This method helps speed up the tenderising process.

SPICE-BASED MARINADES: make quick and easy marinades before cooking portions of poultry, fillets of fish or pork. Pour the oil into a dish and add a pinch of curry powder, a little grated fresh ginger, three pinches of white pepper and a chopped shallot. Marinate the meat or fish for 20 minutes.

YOGHURT-BASED MARINADES: are used for adding flavour and for tenderising white meats such as poultry, veal and fillet of pork. To one portion of yoghurt, add two teaspoons of grated ginger, four sprigs of chopped chives, a pinch of salt and three turns of the pepper mill. Mix the pieces of meat with the marinade, cover and leave in the refrigerator to marinate for four hours.

Cleaning wood

Vinegar added to water containing bleach can be used to clean wooden spoons, forks and spatulas.

Marinated salmon fillets

Marinate fresh salmon fillets and enjoy them served with whipped fromage blanc, seasoned with a little powdered ginger.

Serves 4:
- 2 salmon fillets
- 1 handful rock salt
- 1 large onion chopped
- 2 carrots cut into rounds
- 2 bay leaves
- 10 black peppercorns
- 1 clove
- 10 coriander seeds
- 4 tablespoons olive oil
- 4 tablespoons rape seed oil

Rub the salmon fillets with the rock salt and leave them in the refrigerator for six hours, then wash the fillets and immerse them in a marinade made from the remaining ingredients. Salmon fillets preserved in this marinade will keep for several weeks, provided they are stored in sealed preserving bottles in a cool place.

HERBS, SEASONINGS, SPICES & CONDIMENTS

AROMATIC PLANTS, GROWN IN A MEDICINAL PLANT OR HERB GARDEN, WERE ORIGINALLY CULTIVATED FOR THEIR HEALTH GIVING PROPERTIES. TODAY MODERN COOKS INCORPORATE THESE HERBS INTO THEIR RECIPES TO ADD FLAVOUR TO SAUCES, SOUPS AND OTHER DISHES. FOR CENTURIES SPICES HAVE BEEN VALUED MORE HIGHLY THAN GOLD! THEY FEATURE PROMINENTLY IN OUR DAY-TO-DAY COOKING, AND WE COULDN'T MANAGE WITHOUT THEIR FRAGRANCES.

Pesto

This sauce is much better if you use a pestle and mortar instead of a processor to grind the ingredients. Covered in oil, pesto keeps perfectly in the refrigerator.

Serves 4:
- 1 bunch of basil
- 1 clove garlic
- 1 tablespoon pine nuts
- 3 tablespoons olive oil
- 1 oz/25 g parmesan
- pinch salt

Pick off the basil leaves and discard the stalks. Peel the garlic and crush in a mortar, gradually fold in the pine nuts, basil leaves, parmesan, pounding continuously; finally add the olive oil. Salt to taste.

HERBS

BASIL: should preferably be used fresh. Basil loses its aromatic properties when cooked for too long, so it is best added at the last moment to slow-cooking dishes. The same applies to tarragon.

■ One of the best ways to enjoy basil is to sprinkle the leaves on a chilled gazpacho and it is always popular used on a salad of sliced tomatoes and mozzarella.

CHIVES: add flavour to butter by blending it with chopped chives (see page 96).

■ Small bunches of chives dotted around the dish as a garnish for salads or fish are far more decorative than chopped chives.

CORIANDER: this delicate herb is also called Chinese parsley or Arabian parsley. It is particularly useful for preparing tuna tartare or for adding flavour to marinades for raw fish dishes.

TARRAGON: there's nothing tastier for large shellfish, such as lobster or crayfish, or fillets of white fish than a simple topping of tarragon butter and chopped shallots.

MINT: chop finely before adding to gazpacho, a green salad or to cucumber, just before serving.

■ Mint is ideal for enhancing the flavour of strawberries, sorbets and strawberry fruit salads.

■ During the summer, tie up several bunches of mint and place them around the kitchen or dining room as mint keeps mosquitoes at bay.

PARSLEY: flatleaf parsley has a better flavour than the curly variety.

■ Only the leaves are used in recipes; the stalks tend to be discarded. Instead, store the stalks in the refrigerator, and

Keeping herbs fresh

You can keep chopped herbs, covered in olive oil and stored in sealed preserving jars, in the refrigerator for up to a week. Bunches of fresh herbs will last for a few days wrapped in a damp tea towel and stored carefully in the vegetable compartment of the refrigerator.

when you have enough – say three or four bunches – make a quick stock out of the chopped stalks, adding a little onion and a chicken stock cube.

■ Parsley leaves, fried in oil for a few seconds, make a very tasty – and decorative – accompaniment for white meat. Try this with sage and basil leaves, too.

SAGE: goes well with pork, game and veal. You can also use it to flavour the water when cooking pulses.

■ Sprinkle a few fresh sage leaves in hot cooking oil. They will add not only flavour but also a delicious crunchiness to fried potatoes.

■ You cannot fail to amaze your friends if you serve up sage fritters with aperitifs. Coat the leaves in a light fritter batter (see page 135), fry them briefly in very hot oil, drain and serve immediately.

■ Sage's digestive and health-giving properties make it ideal for infusions. According to the old proverb, 'He who has sage in his garden has no need of a doctor.'

VERBENA: it might be thought that verbena and peaches make unusual partners, yet they go marvellously well together. Line the bottom of a steamer with verbena leaves, place peeled peach halves on top, and cook for ten minutes. Add a few verbena leaves, a little sugar and honey to the water used for cooking, put in the peaches and finish cooking them over a gentle heat, stirring them in the syrup for five minutes or so.

HYSSOP: the fragrance of this highly aromatic herb mellows with drying. Use it to add flavour to pork paté or to the gravy made from roast game juices.

■ Apart from tasting superb, light infusions of hyssop will also help you digest a rather heavy meal.

THYME, BAY AND ROSEMARY: should be dried with their heads hanging downwards. Crush all three herbs together and store in a preserving jar in the dark.

■ A bay leaf broken into two pieces gives off more flavour than a leaf left whole.

■ A bay leaf is as essential to tomato sauce as it is to marinades for red meat.

■ To add flavour to potatoes, cut a small slit in each potato and wedge a bay leaf into it, before baking them in their skins, in the oven.

Frozen herb cubes

Store chopped herbs frozen in cubes: finely chop coriander, basil, parsley or chervil, fill the individual sections of an ice tray or a plastic egg box, top with water or cover with olive oil and place in the freezer. Add one or more frozen cubes to your soups, roasts or use for seasoning a salad or steamed vegetables.

Chopped herbs

Chop herbs with a very sharp knife or use a pair of scissors; this releases the flavour better than using a processor.

■ Fruit kept in a storeroom will last longer if bay leaves are placed next to them, as the smell keeps insects away.

■ Place a bouquet of thyme in pumpkin soup for the last 15 minutes of cooking to bring out the flavour. Before serving, strain the soup through a small conical strainer to remove the sprigs of thyme.

■ Infusions made with thyme and rosemary aid digestion.

BOUQUET GARNI: traditionally bouquet garni consists of sprigs of thyme and parsley with a few bay leaves. Add a bouquet garni, the green parts of a leek and a stalk of celery to enhance the flavour of stock.

SEASONINGS

GARLIC: releases its flavour better, and is more digestible, if it is grated or crushed rather than just cut into slices. Garlic is also more digestible if you remove the pithy centre.

■ If the smell lingers on your hands after peeling garlic, rinse them in a solution of water and vinegar.

■ Make the most of spring garlic as it has a particularly delicate flavour.

■ Rub round the inside of your cooking dishes with a garlic clove, cut in two. This adds flavour to the food without masking the taste.

■ Garnish roast leg of lamb or poultry with whole heads of unpeeled garlic, cut in two widthways, and wedged around and under the meat as it cooks.

■ Fried foie gras, roast lamb and poached cod, among other dishes, will benefit from the use of a little garlic purée during preparation. Place the garlic bulbs in the basket of a steamer and cook for about 15 minutes. Remove the pulp by pressing down firmly on each clove, one by one, with your fingers. Add a pinch of salt, a drizzle of olive oil, and blend until reduced to a purée.

ONION: contains a sulphurated extract that irritates the eyes during peeling. Stop your eyes from running by soaking the onions, beforehand, in a solution of warm water and vinegar; alternatively peel the onions under running water.

■ After peeling onions, rub your hands in a solution of water and vinegar or lemon juice to remove the highly clinging odour of these bulbs.

■ To reduce the pungency of onions, blanch them first in boiling water for a minute before browning lightly in a frying pan.

Fishing out herbs

Tie the stalks of your bouquet garni together with string, or wrap the ingredients in a muslin bag (or use a tea ball strainer) to avoid having to fish out the herbs one by one from a stock or casserole.

Follow the example of our grandmothers, and attach the end of the bouquet garni string to the handle of the pan to make it really easy to remove.

Crystallised verbena

Crystallised verbena adds both flavour and sweetness to fruit salads and infusions. Although crystallised verbena is available in shops, making it yourself is easy and great fun. First dry the verbena leaves in a low oven, then soak in a thick sugar syrup before grilling until the sugar crystallises.

■ To fry onions without burning them, lightly coat them in potato flour before placing in hot oil.

■ Add an onion studded with two or three cloves to cabbage soup, boiled chicken or to the water for cooking lentils – the flavour will be superb. Remember to discard the onion before serving.

■ Replace the white wine ingredient in onion soup with either madeira or port; these fortified wines blend particularly well when cooked with onions.

■ Don't throw away onions that have started to sprout; instead chop up the small green shoots and use them to season salads, fried eggs, or an omelette. If you keep the root base of an onion in water (in a hyacinth bulb bowl, for example), the young shoots produced can be used all year round instead of chives.

■ To add colour to stock, place some onion skins in a muslin bag and add to the liquid.

SPICES

■ Spices should be stored in a dry place away from the light. Buy them in small quantities to avoid having spices that have lost some, or all, of their flavour.

■ Heat coriander seeds, Szechwan pepper and sesame seeds in a frying pan for a few seconds before peeling to draw out their full flavour.

CINNAMON: when using cinnamon sticks, crush them to release their fragrance, and wrap them in muslin, or a tea ball strainer, so that the bits don't get into the mixture.

■ Instead of dusting a fruit tart with cinnamon, add a teaspoonful of ground cinnamon to the dry ingredients before making the pastry. You can improve the flavour of a chocolate cake with cinnamon in the same way. This spice can also be used to flavour rice pudding or crème caramel, or to enhance the taste of a tagine or blanquette of lamb.

VANILLA: to get the best results from vanilla pods, with their marvellous aroma, split them in half and scoop out the small black seeds before adding both the pods and the seeds to your mixture.

■ Prepare your own vanilla sugar by storing a vanilla pod, cut into strips, in a jar of caster sugar.

■ Add a little vanilla to savoury dishes such as blanquette of veal, cockles, squid or foie gras.

An anti-rust agent

Prevent knives from rusting by rubbing them with the flesh of half an onion, dipped in rock salt.

Preserving fresh garlic

To keep garlic fresh for several weeks, peel the cloves, place them in an attractive preserving jar and cover them in oil.

ANISE: comes ground or as seeds. Wrap ground anise in muslin before adding it to the other ingredients, to prevent the bits from getting into the mixture.

■ Add one or two aniseeds to the boiling water when cooking lentils, also to stewed apple or a herbal tea infusion for a delicious spicy flavour.

STAR ANISE: is popular in Chinese cooking, use it ground or whole with fruit.

NUTMEG: using a fine nutmeg grater, freshly grate and add to mulled wine, baked apples or pears cooked in wine. You can also use it to enhance the flavour of mashed potatoes or homemade pâté.

CLOVES: stick a clove into a whole, peeled onion and add to soup. For extra fragrance, add an onion and clove to the water when cooking rice.

■ The pungent aroma of crushed clove will enhance the flavour of peaches poached in wine, chocolate cakes and other gateaux.

■ Our grandmothers were familiar with the versatility of this spice, which is an excellent antiseptic. To benefit from its health-giving properties, pop a clove and the juice of half a lemon into some boiling water, and drink the infusion.

CUMIN: for improved fragrance, you're better off buying the whole seeds and grinding them yourself in a blender.

■ This spice is particularly good at bringing out the flavours of soft white yoghurt-style cheeses. You can also use cumin to flavour glazed carrots and fried or steamed courgettes.

CURRY: the type of curry powder with which we are all familiar is actually a blend of several different spices. It comes in various 'strengths', which are described on the packaging. Choose a medium or strong curry powder for making vinaigrette dressings, sauces and vegetable soups made from courgette, leek and potato; use a mild curry powder to season fresh goat's cheese and fruit salads.

■ Blend curry spices with oil and use the paste to coat meat. Leave it to marinate for at least an hour before cooking.

LIQUORICE: infused in milk lends a marvellous fragrance not only to cream desserts and cakes, but also to syrups and coulis.

Flavoured sugars

For enhanced flavour, add a cinnamon stick to your sugar bowl. You can do the same with vanilla pods.

Subtle mace nutmeg

If you buy whole nutmegs with their husks of mace intact from a delicatessen, and you have a powerful blender, you can try removing the mace covering and grind the fibrous threads. This is how you obtain nutmeg mace with its subtle fragrance of orange peel; use for flavouring marinades and stewed fruits. Otherwise buy the mace ready ground.

■ Add a stick of liquorice to the sauce when cooking game such as pigeon or duck.

MIXED SPICE: consists of a blend of cinnamon, nutmeg, cloves and ground ginger. Although commonly used in cakes and pastries – add a pinch to the dry ingredients when making shortbread – it is equally effective for preparing cooked meats, stews, stocks or marinades.

FIVE SPICE POWDER: this blend of Asian spices is made up of star anise, Szechwan pepper, fennel seeds, cloves and cinnamon. As well as being used in Chinese cookery, a pinch or two peps up cake mixtures, fruit compotes and enhances the flavour of meat and poultry marinades.

SAFFRON: is used to enhance the flavour of custard or pears cooked in wine. It also adds that *je ne sais quoi*, a certain sweetness and aroma to tomato sauce. Although classified as a spice, strictly speaking saffron is a herb!

ESPELETTE PEPPER: this powder, made from a ground red pepper, is highly aromatic. It is often used instead of black pepper, in southwest France where it is produced.
■ Use it in savoury dishes, and more specifically in patés, cabbage soup, piperade (an omelette-style dish) and squid and fish-based dishes. It's perfect for drawing out the flavour of courgette gratin, which tends to be rather bland, and for garnishing and adding a delicious flavour to fried eggs and pumpkin soup.
■ Used sparingly, it lends an exotic taste to chocolate-based recipes.

PEPPER: pre-ground it becomes stale very quickly and all that remains are its tannins. It is therefore advisable always to grind peppercorns yourself and add towards the end of the cooking process.
■ Black peppercorns are immature berries with their husks. Choose large peppercorns and grind in a quality pepper mill. You could also grind together some rock salt and pepper (three parts salt to one part pepper), an excellent mixture that is particularly useful for salting foie gras.
■ White pepper is made from mature berries without their husks. It keeps well left whole and should be ground immediately before use.
■ Szechwan pepper is highly aromatic and adds a festive touch to the seasoning of foie gras terrine, as well as to fried foie gras.

Release the seeds!

Prise open some cardamom pods just wide enough to release the small, black, aromatic seeds from inside. Discard the pods and use the seeds to flavour, among other dishes, smoked fish and curries.

Saffron aromas

Reducing saffron strands to a powder makes this spice more aromatic. To do so, heat an empty pan, turn off the heat, arrange the strands over the bottom of the pan and leave for a few seconds before grinding them using a pestle and mortar. Add the ground saffron to recipes, as required.

It also gives a marvellous aroma to fish cooked in foil. Before use, heat in a frying pan for a minute and then whiz in a grinder. You can also mix it with salt for flavouring fish.

■ Improve fish marinades with a few whole Java long pepper kernels.

SALT: causes a chemical reaction when cooked with other food ingredients that is not always desirable, therefore the point at which salt is added is important. Always add salt to meat when the dish is half-cooked or once cooking is complete; salt the water for green beans and pasta when it reaches boiling point, and season sautéed potatoes with salt at the very last minute.

■ A few grains of rice placed in a saltcellar will absorb humidity from the atmosphere and prevent the salt from becoming damp.

■ Remove traces of rust from white linen by applying a combination of lemon juice and salt.

■ A mixture of rock salt and vinegar can be used to de-scale kettles and saucepans that are coated with limescale deposits.

CONDIMENTS

CAPERS: mix capers with ground salt and softened butter to make caper butter. This highly aromatic mixture goes well with calves' liver and fish fillets.

■ You can substitute capers with the flower buds of organically grown plants, such as marigolds, nasturtiums or dandelions which have a slightly bitter taste.

GHERKINS: don't wash gherkins intended for pickling, instead rub them with rock salt in a tea towel to remove the prickles. Add a few coriander seeds, tarragon leaves and a lump of sugar to the preserving jar.

■ When buying gherkins, drain off the vinegar and refill the jars with your own aromatic vinegar (see page 17) adding a few peppercorns, a shallot and a clove of garlic to the pickle jar.

GINGER: dries out very quickly, so it is worth storing it in a sealed preserving jar in the refrigerator or in the freezer – you can grate the ginger while it is still frozen. If you immerse ginger in sherry, it will keep for a month or so in the refrigerator.

■ Ginger is perfect for drawing out the flavours of chicken with chicory, a quince tagine or a fish marinade.

A different salt for every dish

Flavour salt with herbs or spices and store in tightly sealed preserving jars where it will last for several weeks. Sprinkle a mixture of salt and crushed hazelnuts over fresh anchovy fillets; season salads and crudités with salt mixed with toasted sesame seeds; sprinkle rosemary and thyme-flavoured salt over grilled white and red meats.

■ Small pieces of crystallised ginger are ideal for flavouring chocolate cake.

■ Stem ginger offers excellent digestive benefits: you can also prepare an infusion from finely sliced pieces of root ginger.

OLIVES: store for several months, covered in olive oil, in jars. You can improve the flavour of olives by adding a few sprigs of thyme, savory and oregano to the jar.

■ For an effective way of removing salt from olives stored in brine, blanch them first for a few minutes before adding to recipes such as bread, salad or tagine.

■ Tapenade — a paste made from black or green olives — is handy for garnishing and enhancing all sorts of dishes. Served on bite-size pieces of toast it also makes a delicious accompaniment to aperitifs.

FRENCH MUSTARD: keep in the refrigerator because mustard doesn't like the light. If it dries out you can resurrect it by mixing in a tablespoon of vinegar and a little added sugar.

■ For a better blend, when adding mustard to a sauce, fold it into the mixture away from the heat.

■ Make your own flavoured mustard by adding the flavouring of your choice — chopped herbs, shallot, lemon or saffron.

ENGLISH MUSTARD: keeps well in powdered form and should be made up as needed using cold water.

Ring the changes!

When serving a beef stew, offer your guests a selection of different mustards as accompaniments – mustard mixed with wine, violet, cassis, etc. They will give this homely dish an air of sophistication. These mustards will also bring out the flavour of cauliflower, potatoes, carrots and steamed turnips.

Tapenade

This olive paste is mixed with olive oil and usually seasoned with anchovies, capers, herbs and garlic. If you don't have any black olives to hand use green olives instead. It's equally delicious!

Serves 4:
- 7 oz/200 g olive paste
- 4 or 5 anchovy fillets in olive oil
- 1 tablespoon capers
- 4 gherkins
- 1 clove garlic crushed
- 3 twists of the pepper mill

Place all the ingredients in a blender and reduce to a coarse purée. It's a good idea to add a few drops of water, but this is optional.

■ Cook tied in bunches, or in an oval shaped casserole, to prevent the asparagus from disintegrating.

■ Warm asparagus served on fingers of bread makes a splendid accompaniment for soft-boiled eggs.

COURGETTES: don't peel young courgettes because the vitamins are concentrated in their skins.

■ Courgettes tend to have a rather bland flavour, so feel free to spice them up a bit with cumin, cinnamon, turmeric, ginger or pepper.

■ An original way to serve courgettes is to cut them into very thin strips, plunge into boiling water, and cook for one minute. Then add them to pasta dishes topped with a dash of olive oil.

■ Whole young courgettes cut into very thin slices or strips, drizzled with olive oil and lemon juice and sprinkled with freshly grated parmesan are a real treat.

■ At markets, you may come across what are known as courgette flowers – very small courgettes with the flower heads still attached. Dip them whole in fritter batter and fry to enjoy as an accompaniment for aperitifs.

CHICORY: choose chicory that is a very pale, verging on yellow, colour. If you notice red or brownish marks on the outer leaves, leave well alone because this is an indication that the chicory is not that fresh. The bitterness of this plant is concentrated in its root so it makes sense to hollow out the cone-shaped centre, to reduce the bitterness.

■ Don't soak or cook chicory in water as it only accentuates its bitterness. Instead, cook chicory by steaming or braise it in a little lemon juice with a pinch of sugar for caramelising.

CARROTS: contain a high concentration of vitamin A; eat them with oil for increased vitamin absorption.

■ Cut carrots thinly into strips lengthways and cook in a frying pan with a little butter and chopped garlic until they are slightly softened, but still firm. Sprinkle with freshly chopped parsley immediately before serving.

■ Grated carrot tastes better seasoned with vinegar; it also goes perfectly mixed with garlic and olive oil, raisins and pine kernels. Prepare at the very last minute so that it looks fresh and crunchy, rather than tired, as if it's been left standing for too long. A few drops of orange blossom water and some orange

Shredded chicory

Chicory doesn't go well in salads because it discolours easily. Better to serve it separately, shredded lengthways, sprinkled with lemon juice and olive oil and garnished with grated apple and chopped walnut kernels.

Rock salt for young carrots

Don't peel spring carrots, just place them in a tea towel, add a generous handful of rock salt and rub together. You'll save time and you won't end up with yellow fingers.

juice added to the seasoning will give grated carrot dishes an exotic flavour.

■ When preparing braised carrots, add a pinch of sugar to caramelise and a little cumin for flavour.

LEEKS: don't throw away the green leaves of leeks, instead, tie them together with string and use them to flavour stock, or to add to your bouquet garni.

■ Instead of serving leeks with vinaigrette, simply cook them in water with a glass of dry white wine added, drain, add a knob of butter and season with paprika and coriander.

CELERIAC: choose decent-sized, firm celeriac. Take care, in winter, because celeriac sometimes has two outer layers, in which case you'll need to peel it twice.

■ Before cooking, add a little lemon juice to retain its white colour.

POTATOES: choose firm, shoot-free potatoes with smooth, unblemished skins. Store potatoes in a cool, dark place. Potatoes are the only vegetables that don't lose their vitamin content when exposed to air.

■ Don't peel new potatoes, simply rub them with rock salt in a tea towel, instead.

■ Different varieties of potatoes are better suited to different methods of preparation. Choose waxy varieties such as Belle de Fontenay or La Ratte for potato gratins and salads; floury potatoes such as King Edward for mashed or baked potatoes and Maris Piper for boiling or roasting. Floury potatoes are also good for purée, chips or roast potatoes.

■ When boiling potatoes, they should be of a uniform size and cooked whole. Add a handful of rock salt to the water to prevent disintegration during cooking; season with a bay leaf and keep an eye on the pan!

■ Coconut milk makes a pleasant alternative to cow's milk in a gratin dauphinois.

■ Prepare a potato salad and, while it's still warm, sprinkle with a glass of white wine and mix gently so as not to crush the potatoes: the resulting salad will be particularly smooth.

■ If sauté potatoes are precooked in a steamer before being browned in a frying pan, they absorb less oil and develop a much browner, crispier appearance. Whichever method is used, add the salt at the last moment.

Traditional mashed potato

This recipe simply involves mashing the potatoes and butter with a fork, then softening them with a little boiling milk and putting them through a vegetable mouli. You can replace the butter with olive oil or, alternatively, with some olive purée or tapenade.

Violet potato crisps for aperitifs

Make your own crisps using Vitelotte potatoes with their skins left on. Cut the potatoes as thinly as possible using a mandolin slicer and deep fry in vegetable oil preheated to 250°F/130°C until light, golden brown.

- Before cooking potatoes in the oven, cut them in half and leave to marinate in rosemary-, thyme- and bay-flavoured olive oil, for an hour.
- Instead of using the usual frying oil to make chips try replacing it with goose or duck fat. Chip potatoes evenly with a good kitchen knife, rinse, dry and cook in the preheated fat, at 315°F/160°C, for ten minutes; drain the chips and then finish frying at 350°F/180°C until they are nice and crisp.
- Add a few sage leaves to the boiling fat used for deep-frying chips or for sautéing potatoes. Not only will sage add flavour and a hint of fruitiness, but the potatoes will also be much crisper and more deliciously crunchy.
- To eliminate the smell of frying, add a sprig of parsley to the hot oil.

CAULIFLOWER: gives off a strong smell during cooking and this can be minimised by adding a crust of bread pierced with a clove and a generous squirt of vinegar to the cooking water.

CABBAGE: green cabbage should have a good head and a bold green colour. Don't keep cabbage for long – cook as soon as possible after purchase.
- Don't overcook cabbage; the longer it cooks, the stronger its smell and the less digestible it becomes.
- Enjoy steam-cooked cabbage warm, drizzled with a quality wine vinegar and some olive oil and sprinkled with chives or chopped parsley.
- Use thinly sliced, raw white cabbage which has been marinated in olive oil, in salads. There is only one proviso – it must be exceedingly fresh.

PUMPKIN: to pep up jaded pumpkin, season with Espelette pepper and nutmeg.
- If you're on a diet, don't feel guilty about making yourself a smooth pumpkin soup, because this vegetable is very low in calories (avoid adding any potatoes to this low-calorie soup).
- Keep the pumpkin seeds to toast in a frying pan and offer as accompaniments for aperitifs, or scatter them over a dish of pumpkin purée, immediately before serving.

CHINESE CABBAGE (CHINESE LEAVES): we tend only to use the middle ribbed parts of Chinese cabbage, and we're not quite sure what to do with its green leaves. However,

Really white cauliflower

Choose a very white cauliflower, well-rounded, firm and free of brown blemishes. Wash quickly in a solution of water and vinegar; then sprinkle with lemon juice to preserve its colour while cooking.

Pumpkin gratin

Rather more inspiring than a smooth soup, pumpkin makes a very fine gratin. Adding anchovies can revive a vegetable that is past its best, without adding extra calories.

Serves 4:
- 3lb 5oz/1.5 kg pumpkin
- 2 chopped onions
- 3 anchovies soaked to remove the salt
- 2 tablespoons oil
- breadcrumbs or grated crusts
- salt, pepper

Dice the pumpkin and place in a stewing pot with the chopped onions and cover with water. Cook over a gentle heat until all the water has evaporated. Transfer the mixture to a buttered gratin dish and add some crushed anchovies. Sprinkle breadcrumbs or grated crusts on top, season and cook for 15 minutes in the oven at 350°F/180°C/gas mark 4.

Beetroot purée

*To accompany white meats,
substitute the ubiquitous carrot
purée with a beetroot purée.*

Serves 4:
- 2 raw beetroots
- 1 clove garlic
- 1 onion chopped
- 1 tomato crushed
- 2 tablespoons red wine vinegar
- salt, pepper
- 1 tablespoon thick crème fraîche

Peel and dice the beetroots; place in a saucepan; add the garlic, chopped onion, crushed tomato, red wine vinegar and season with salt and pepper. Cook over a gentle heat for 20 minutes, until the beetroot is tender. Finally, add the crème fraîche and mix together.

Chinese cabbage leaves that have been coarsely chopped and precooked in a frying pan make a perfect extra ingredient for pie fillings; they can also be used instead of spinach leaves to wrap sardines and anchovies before cooking in foil, in the oven.

■ Cook midribs in plenty of water, which has been only slightly salted as Chinese cabbage absorbs a huge amount of salt. Lightly brown in a frying pan with a little lard and sprinkle with Espelette pepper to bring out the flavour.

GLOBE ARTICHOKES: to check out the freshness of an artichoke, bend a leaf. If it doesn't break then the artichoke is very fresh, so go ahead and buy it.

■ This vegetable blackens very quickly, so do not to cut it up until the last minute and add a few drops of lemon juice to the water used for cooking.

■ After cooking, artichokes should be eaten within 12 hours, otherwise they oxidise and may become toxic.

FRENCH BEANS: watch the cooking time of French beans as they cook through very quickly. Salt the water once it's boiling, add the beans and cook uncovered.

■ Immerse the beans in cold water containing ice cubes, immediately after cooking to retain their fresh, green colour. Bicarbonate of soda also helps to keep their colour but it does soften the beans.

BEETROOT: is best cooked in the oven, wrapped in greaseproof paper, or cooked in a pressure cooker. Note that beetroot takes at least two hours to cook in the oven, at 350°F/180°C/gas mark 4. These two methods are much better than just boiling beetroot in water.

■ Try this unusual way to enjoy beetroot. Peel; sauté in a frying pan with half butter, half oil until cooked but still firm and sprinkle with a little nutmeg before serving.

GARDEN PEAS: as ingredients for a ragout, peas must be very young and tender. Braise in a whole lettuce, finely shredded, instead of water. Finally, add some salted belly pork cut into small pieces, a teaspoonful of sugar and two knobs of butter.

■ Don't prepare a purée of garden peas using a blender; use a vegetable mouli instead and the resulting purée will be smoother.

Healthy toast bites

Smoked fish like salmon, taramasalata, tapenade or anchovy butter and sliced horseradish all make suitable toppings for bite-sized toasted bread snacks.

LETTUCE: revive a slightly wilting lettuce by dipping it first in lukewarm water, followed by chilled water. A squirt of vinegar in the water used to wash lettuce will remove any unwanted creepy-crawlies. Finally, if you want to keep lettuce fresh for a while, wash, spin lightly in a salad-spinner, wrap in a damp tea towel and store in the vegetable compartment of your refrigerator.

■ Liven up lettuce and endive by mixing them with a selection of other varieties of salad leaves such as lamb's lettuce, rocket, dandelion and red endive. Add some young spinach shoots and spice up the salad dressing with curry powder, chopped shallots or a few garlic croutons. Try using a variety of vinegars and oils in the dressing.

■ Don't throw away slightly bruised or withered lettuce leaves — they can be used to replace the water for braising garden peas. You can also add them to the ingredients for making vegetable soup, or braise them with a little salted lard.

TOMATOES: should have shiny, smooth skins, and bright green stalks. Don't store tomatoes in the refrigerator, and only wash them just before using so that they retain their full flavour. Tomatoes grown outdoors, produced between the end of July and the first frosts, have the best, real tomato flavour.

■ To make light work of peeling ripe tomatoes, boil first for two minutes; then chill immediately in cold water.

■ When cooking tomatoes, make sure you choose the size and type of tomato appropriate to your chosen recipe. Large Marmande tomatoes are ideal for stuffing and oblong Roma tomatoes make very good preserves. Simply halve, sprinkle with rock salt and bake in the oven, at 225°F/110°C/gas mark ¼ for six hours, then store in preserving jars, covered in olive oil. Fleshy, slightly watery beefsteak tomatoes are ideal sliced for salads. Finally, cherry tomatoes make an excellent accompaniment for fried meat and fish dishes if added to the frying pan with a few chopped shallots and, of course, they can always be relied upon to garnish a cold buffet.

■ To cook tomatoes in the oven, cut a criss-cross shape into the top of each tomato and insert a mixture of olive oil, crushed garlic and rock salt into the centre; cook in the oven at 350°F/180°C /gas mark 4 for at least 30 minutes.

■ Before preparing a tomato tart or quiche, first make sure that you leave the sliced tomatoes, preferably salted, to drain in a colander, for about 30 minutes, to draw out the excess liquid.

Spring salad

Garnish your salads just before serving with edible flowers such as nasturtiums, which have a delicious flavour, marigolds, violets and thyme blossom.

Tomato granita

Make your own tomato granita by freezing cooked tomato coulis. Crush and flake with a fork before it is fully frozen and enjoy as a starter with some slices of good country ham.

AUBERGINES: choose small shiny aubergines – larger ones always contain more seeds.

■ To remove the bitterness of aubergines, cut into thick slices, soak in milk sprinkled with rock salt and leave in this solution for at least two hours.

■ Fried aubergines absorb a lot of oil. To counteract this, dip the slices in egg white and blitz in the microwave first, before cooking in the oil. Gratin dishes will be lighter if you pre-cook the aubergines in a steamer, for a few minutes, beforehand.

■ Baked aubergine is delicious and quick to prepare. Allow one small, unpeeled aubergine cut lengthways into quarters, per person. Top with olive oil, rock salt and chopped garlic and place in the oven at 350°F/180°C /gas mark 4 and cook for 20 minutes.

PEPPERS: whatever the recipe, peppers are better with their somewhat indigestible skins removed. Roast in the oven or over an open flame, then wrap in kitchen paper and chill them, to make peeling easier. If the skins are thick enough you can peel peppers using a paring knife.

AVOCADOS: to avoid damaging the flesh, cut avocados in half with their skins on. Remove the stone using the tip of a knife; then ease the flesh away from the skins with a tablespoon.

■ To ripen avocados under the right conditions, buy them while still very firm, wrap in newspaper and store until the skins are soft to the touch.

■ Drizzle a dash of lemon juice on to the flesh of avocados to prevent blackening.

CUCUMBERS: those grown outdoors often tend to be slightly bitter. To counter this bitterness, cut the cucumbers into strips and soak in milk for an hour before seasoning.

SPINACH: avoid cooking in water. To improve liquid retention for tastier spinach, cook in a frying pan with a little butter or oil. Fresh spinach should be eaten as soon as possible after purchase. Set aside young spinach shoots for garnishing salads.

TRUFFLES: can be stored in the freezer for six to eight months, in small glass jars covered in groundnut oil, or wrapped in aluminium foil. You can also cover them in olive oil and sterilise.

Radish-top soup

Don't throw away young radish-tops because they make a delicious soup. Add a few herbs, one or two potatoes and a vegetable stock cube.

Criss-cross radishes

Choose firm radishes and cut a criss-cross shape at the base of each radish to act as pincers for holding butter and salt – both these ingredients go well with radishes.

MUSHROOMS

■ Don't wash wild mushrooms, as they'll lose all their flavour. Instead, clean with absorbent paper and scrape any discolouration from the stalks using a small paring knife.

CEP MUSHROOMS: should be cooked very gently as they absorb a lot of oil during cooking. Most of the excess oil can be absorbed by adding a piece of bread with the crust removed to the pan, during the final stage of cooking.

■ A few highly aromatic dried cep mushrooms added while simmering, will certainly perk up the flavour of a meat casserole.

■ Use the water left over from soaking dried mushrooms to make a sauce or soup.

■ Firm, young cep mushrooms can be eaten raw. Cut them into thin slices using a mandolin food slicer, season with salt and a dash of olive oil and garnish sparingly with shavings of parmesan.

BUTTON MUSHROOMS: wash rapidly in a solution of water and vinegar to remove all impurities.

■ This variety of mushrooms tends to blacken quickly, so sprinkle generously with lemon juice if serving raw.

■ If you immerse button mushrooms in boiling water for a few seconds they won't split when you skewer them.

PULSES

■ Apart from lentils and split peas, dried vegetables, such as beans and chickpeas, should be soaked overnight. If you forget or do not have time you can blanch them instead. Cover the pulses with cold water, bring to the boil, remove immediately from the heat and drain. Repeat this process twice, changing the water each time, before continuing with the actual cooking process. The exception is kidney beans, which must be soaked for about eight hours and then boiled fast in clean water for at least 10 minutes to remove toxins in the skins.

■ Certain rules apply when cooking dried vegetables. Firstly, try to use soft water, low in mineral salts which toughen dried vegetables. If your water is hard, add a pinch of bicarbonate of soda. Finally, once you've covered the dried vegetables in cold, unsalted water, cook over a sufficiently moderate heat to prevent the skins from splitting.

A very refined oil

Never throw away the preserving oil when you've eaten all the truffles. It comes in very handy for flavouring dishes including salads, pasta or steamed vegetables.

Storage in jars or the freezer

Pre-cook cep mushrooms in a frying pan and store them in preserving jars, covered with oil. Very fresh, firm cep mushrooms will also store well in the freezer.

- For best results when reducing vegetables to a purée, use a vegetable mouli because this will give a rougher texture than an electric blender.
- Leftovers of lentil, bean or chickpea purée make a good base for soup – just add a chicken stock cube. You could serve the soup with croutons rubbed in garlic.
- Always ensure that pulses used for making preserves are rinsed thoroughly beforehand, to remove the starch.

DRIED BEANS: even beans meant to be served warm will benefit from a dash of vinegar.

LENTILS: should be rinsed before cooking. They take the least time of all pulses so add them to soups and stews.
- When preparing lentil salad, season well in advance (the lentils will be much more tender and tasty). Bring out the flavour of lentil salad with capers and sliced gherkins.

SPLIT PEAS: when cooking split peas add a few spinach leaves to the water to enhance their colour.
- Use a purée of split peas seasoned with cumin to replace mashed potatoes as a topping for minced lamb shepherd's pie.

CHICKPEAS: blanch twice, then cook in plenty of water. There's only one way to be sure that chickpeas are cooked to perfection, and that's to taste them!
- Cook chickpeas in honey and serve as an accompaniment to roast duck breasts.

Split pea purée

Serve split pea purée in small, individual ramekins. The crème fraîche and butter can be replaced with a clove of garlic blended in olive oil.

Serves 6:
- 10½ oz/300 g split peas
- 2 tablespoons crème fraîche
- ¾ oz/20 g butter
- salt, pepper
- fresh coriander or chervil

Cover the split peas with twice their volume in water and cook until all the liquid has been absorbed. Add the crème fraîche and the butter; season with salt and pepper. Garnish with sprigs of coriander or chervil.

Aroma and smoothness

Add a star anise, one or two sprigs of fennel or a little savory when cooking dried beans. A spoonful of olive oil added to the water used for cooking them gives smoother results.

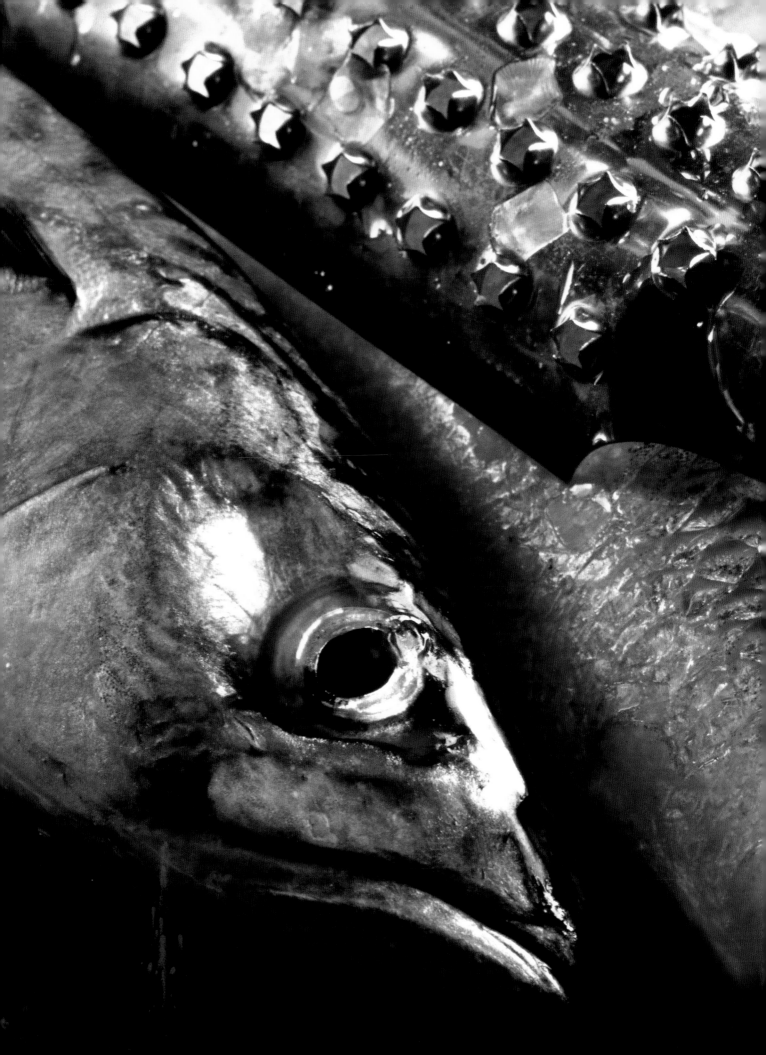

FISH, SHELLFISH & SEAFOOD

IN THE PAST MASTERY OF THE ART OF CURING, DRYING AND SALTING FISH WAS A VERY DESIRABLE SKILL TO POSSESS. THESE PROCESSES ENABLED EVERYONE TO BENEFIT FROM THE EXTRAORDINARY RICHNESS OF THE SEA. MORE RECENTLY RAPID MEANS OF TRANSPORT AND NOUVELLE CUISINE HAVE CHANGED AND SHAPED OUR PRESENT DAY TASTE FOR FISH. WE ENJOY IT FRESH, SOMETIMES RAW, AND WE ADOPT METHODS OF PREPARATION THAT OPTIMISE BOTH ITS FLAVOUR AND ITS NUTRITIONAL PROPERTIES.

FISH

Potted mackerel

Prepare potted mackerel and serve with toasted garlic bread to accompany aperitifs.

Serves 4:
- 2 shallots chopped
- 4 mackerel fillets
- Salt, pepper
- Espelette pepper
- 1 clove garlic chopped
- ⅓ pt/20 cl white wine

Fry the shallots gently in olive oil. Add the mackerel fillets, season with salt, pepper, Espelette pepper and garlic, then sprinkle with the white wine and cook for 10 to 15 minutes. Roughly mash the mackerel flesh with a fork and serve in an attractive dish.

■ To prevent fish from drying out, should you need to store it for a day or two, brush it with olive oil and wrap in cling-film.

■ If you don't possess a fish-scaler, use a scallop shell to remove fish scales, starting from the tail and work towards the head. Never scale fish that you intend to grill or cook in salt, because the scales create a barrier that prevent the flesh from absorbing the salt.

■ Saltwater fish should be washed in salted water, not fresh water, which helps them retain their fresh sea aroma.

■ You can simplify the preparation and cooking of fish if you fillet it first, or ask your fishmonger to fillet it for you. It is much easier to gauge whether filleted fish is cooked than it is when cooking whole fish, and you don't need to worry about attractive presentation on the plate, because this is easy to achieve with filleted fish.

■ To prepare fish fillets, slide a small, serrated knife (or a very sharp-bladed knife) between the backbone and the flesh, working from tail to head. Use a pair of tweezers to remove any small fish bones left behind; find them by running your finger over the fillets, again moving from tail to head.

■ An easy way to cook fish fillets is in the oven. Cover the bottom of the fish dish with a bed of chopped shallots, place the fillets on top, skin facing upwards, dress with olive oil and cook in the oven at 350°F/180°C/gas mark 4, for 10 to 15 minutes, according to thickness.

■ Deep-frozen fish regains its original fresh flavour and texture better if you defrost it in milk in the refrigerator, not at room temperature.

■ The flesh of your fish will be whiter if you sprinkle it with lemon juice before cooking.

■ When grilling or cooking large fish in the oven, score the flesh for more even results.

Truly fresh fish

When choosing fish, to ensure that it is really fresh, check that the skin is shiny, the eyes clear, the gills a clear red colour and that it has the tang of the tide.

■ When marinating raw fish, add the lemon juice at the last minute, either immediately before serving or just before cooking the fish.

■ If you don't have time to prepare a quick fish stock, simply add 1 oz/30 g of rock salt to 1¾ pints/1 litre of water. Cooking a whole fish in stock should start from cold to ensure that the fish flesh remains firm. After cooking, let the fish cool in the liquid to prevent it from drying out.

■ When frying fish, you don't need to add salt until the fish is half cooked, this helps prevent it from sticking to the pan. Fried fish will be crisper if you dip it in milk, before coating it in flour.

■ Steamed fish should be cooked on a bed of lettuce leaves, sorrel or fennel, as this will prevent the boiling water from splashing on to the fish.

■ Keep the heads and backbones after preparing fish such as hake, sea bream, gurnard or sole and use them to make fish stock. Place them in a large saucepan of water containing a sprig of thyme, a bay leaf, a peeled onion studded with a clove, a carrot, some parsley stalks and a chicken stock cube, and simmer for at least an hour to reduce the ingredients. Any fish stock that's surplus to requirements can be stored in small containers in the freezer or in an ice cube tray – it'll come in handy, at a later date.

■ The persistent smell of fish on your hands is very easy to remove; simply rub your hands with the pulp of a lemon or soak them in a solution of water and vinegar.

■ Offer your guests individual finger bowls containing warm water with a few drops of lemon juice added, decorated with a seasonal flower.

■ Wash dishes that have been used for preparing fish in salted water, to remove the persistent smell.

SALTED ANCHOVIES: make an anchovy-based sauce, with added olive oil and a hint of garlic, to enjoy with raw vegetables. This sauce can also be used to deglaze the meat juices from a roast leg of lamb.

MACKEREL: brush with mustard before cooking in the oven to mask its strong taste.

■ Mackerel is a fatty fish and it is easier to digest if you sprinkle it with rock salt and leave to marinate for an hour or two in wine vinegar.

Desalting anchovies

To remove the salt from anchovies, rinse in cold water, then leave to marinate in wine vinegar for at least 15 minutes.

Citrus fruit marinade

Before cooking sardines, or before eating them raw, brush the fillets with a marinade of citrus fruit zests. Make it from the grated rinds of an orange, a lemon and a grapefruit mixed with olive oil. This marinade can also be used for sea bream or mackerel.

TUNA: for smoother flesh, marinate tuna in a marinade of olive oil, shallots, and few drops of vinegar, for at least 15 minutes before cooking.

■ As with meat, this fish benefits from resting for ten minutes or so when the cooking process is complete. This helps retain moisture and prevents the flesh from becoming too dry.

■ Coriander really makes tuna tartare special. Sprinkle the minced tuna with olive oil, add some freshly chopped shallots and coriander and season with salt and pepper.

■ You can tell when tuna is properly cooked, because the flesh comes away from the backbone.

SALMON: retains its pink, fleshy colour better when poached rapidly in water with an added pinch of bicarbonate of soda. Avoid adding vinegar to the water because it spoils the colour of the salmon.

■ To keep smoked salmon moist, soak it in milk or better still steam it for a few minutes.

SOLE: don't eat it too fresh if you want it to lose its elasticity and be more manageable to serve.

RED MULLET: don't de-scale or fillet this fish if you intend cooking it in a frying pan or in the oven, as boneless mullet tends to dry out quickly. Once cooked, the skin and bones are easy to remove.

■ Don't throw away the liver when gutting red mullet, because it is the liver that lends this fish its distinctive flavour.

COD: to cook cod, immerse the fish in a pan of cold water and bring to the boil over a high heat. As soon as the water reaches boiling point, remove from the heat, cover and keep the fish in the liquid for a further 20 minutes to allow it to soften and regain its volume.

■ To whiten cod flesh, poach it in milk before cooking.

SQUID: its characteristic iridescent white colour is an indication of its freshness.

■ Cut squid into strips and fry before adding to a sauce, to remove excess water. Use this liquid to improve the flavour of any sauce, reducing it over a low heat before blending with the sauce. Cook squid slowly to prevent it from becoming tough.

■ Squid ink can be refrigerated for up to three days. Make the most of it by using it to cook rice or pasta.

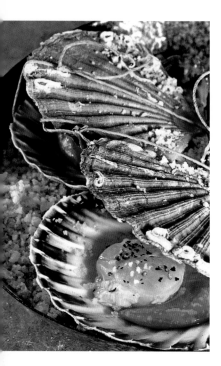

Cooking scallops in their shells

If you've bought whole scallops in their shells the best way to cook them is in the oven. Split the scallop shells open by inserting the point of a knife between the two halves, drizzle a little olive oil on to the contents, season with salt and pepper and close them back together again, tying with a piece of string. Cook for approximately 5 to 7 minutes, at 350°F/180°C/gas mark 4.

Soaking salt cod

The correct method for desalting fish involves placing the fish in a sieve to avoid contact with the deposited salt, then totally immerse the fish in a large bowl of cold water. Choose thick pieces of cod, place them skin face upwards and soak to remove the salt for 24 to 36 hours, changing the water several times.

OCTOPUS: to tenderise, cut into pieces and place in a tea towel with some rock salt and rub briskly. If time permits, fast-freeze octopus, as freezing breaks down the molecules, thus tenderising the flesh.

■ In the Mediterranean, they can tell whether octopus is cooked if the flesh surrounding the thickest tentacles is soft to the touch.

■ Cook octopus with potatoes. When the potatoes are cooked, so too is the octopus.

Fragile, beware!

As with other shellfish such as spider crab, lobster and saltwater crayfish, crab should not be overcooked because its flesh is very fragile. Twenty minutes should be enough.

SEAFOOD AND SHELLFISH

CRAB: when buying a crab, check that it is heavy enough — a good indication that the crab is nice and plump.

■ In general, male crabs tend to be fleshier than the females which contain roe. The female crab can also be distinguished from the male by the larger fin underneath its belly which is used to carry its eggs.

■ If you're only buying the large claws of a crab, smash the shell with a small hammer or a stone. Fry them in olive oil and rock salt, in a pan with the lid on. Eat crab claws with your fingers.

LOBSTER AND SALTWATER CRAYFISH: if you can't face plunging these live creatures into boiling water, place them in the freezer for 15 minutes beforehand; the cold anaesthetises them and they succumb to cooking without a struggle.

■ Lobster and saltwater crayfish (also called spiny lobster) are best enjoyed simply prepared, topped with tarragon butter (see page 96) or with a sauce produced from the roes contained within the chests of these crustaceans. When cooked, the roes assume a pinkish tinge, hence their name, 'corals'.

PRAWNS AND SHRIMPS: if you're lucky enough to come across live shrimps, snap them up! Sauté them in a frying pan the same day, season with a dash of pastis and enjoy them with an aperitif.

■ Prawns are superb when purchased raw, cooked for three minutes in salted boiling water, and enjoyed still warm.

OYSTERS: always discard the first lot of water, the second is always better.

For the stock!

After soaking whelks and winkles in a mixture of water and vinegar for five minutes, cook them in a simple stock flavoured with herbs and spices – parsley, thyme, a peeled onion studded with a clove – for no more than 15 minutes, otherwise the flesh becomes too rubbery. Then enjoy them with a saffron-flavoured mayonnaise.

■ Oysters can be kept for four or five days in the vegetable compartment of the refrigerator. To store them, arrange side by side and wrap in a damp, linen cloth.

■ A milky-coloured appearance indicates that oysters are in their reproductive phase, but they can still be eaten in this condition and are even more delicious.

■ Enjoy oysters warm, straight from the oven, cooked for two minutes with a spoonful of foie gras and a twist of the pepper mill. To balance oysters while cooking, arrange them in a bed of rock salt on a baking tray.

SCALLOPS: to open easily without using a knife, place them on a baking tray in a pre-heated oven for five minutes and they'll split open as if by magic!

■ Before cooking white scallop flesh, remove the surrounding black strands. Keep the strands and use to make the stock if you intend making a sauce.

■ Fry scallops quickly in butter, for barely a minute. It is absolutely critical that they don't harden or lose their moisture during cooking.

■ If you're planning to serve them as a carpaccio, an easy way to remove the contents of scallops is to leave them in the freezer for ten minutes before preparing. Season with olive oil, salt, pepper, chopped chives and a drop of lemon juice and garnish them with thin strips of lemon rind.

MUSSELS: choose mussels that are shiny and moist, and reject those that are already open.

■ Remove the small filaments known as beards immediately before cooking, so that the mussels don't lose their moisture. To wash mussels, rub them together under cold running water, until the water runs clear. Don't leave mussels soaking in water as they will lose their flavour.

■ Freeze the water in which the mussels were cooked in an ice cube tray; it'll come in handy either as a base for fish stock, or for flavouring fish soup.

CLAMS AND COCKLES: before opening, leave to soak for an hour, in a solution of water and vinegar. Scrub clams thoroughly under running water to remove all traces of sand.

Using a small spoon

Under no circumstances should sea urchins be washed once they are open. Ease out the corals, using a small spoon and just let them melt in your mouth, or toss them into scrambled eggs, just before serving.

MEAT, POULTRY & GAME

ONCE, A MEAL WITHOUT MEAT WAS CONSIDERED INCOMPLETE, BUT TODAY IT PLAYS LESS OF A CENTRAL ROLE IN OUR MEALS. HOWEVER, THE KNOWLEDGE NEEDED TO COOK MEAT WELL AND STORE IT CORRECTLY, AND THE ABILITY TO CHOOSE THE RIGHT CUTS REMAIN ESSENTIAL CULINARY SKILLS. THIS PRIME INGREDIENT SHOULD BE CHOSEN FOR ITS FINE APPEARANCE AND QUALITY, AND TO PREPARE MEAT, AND MORE SPECIFICALLY TO COOK MEAT WELL, IS STILL A TRICKY BUSINESS.

MEAT

Aromatic skewers

Use rosemary twigs, with the leaves removed from three-quarters of their length, as skewers for your kebabs.

- Meat tastes better if it is allowed to mature or 'hang' before being consumed. If it is left for several days after slaughter this will allow the muscles to relax.
- All types of meat should be at room temperature before cooking. The meat will be tenderer if it is removed from the refrigerator at least an hour in advance.
- Choose a dish that's the same size as the meat because any fat given off during cooking burns if it's allowed to spread out in the pan.
- Don't insert garlic cloves into meat because it will lose blood; if you're partial to garlic place a few cloves alongside your roast.
- When cooking meat in the oven, add a small amount of water to the pan, for more succulent flesh.
- Meat should be cooked at a high temperature to start with, 450°F/230°C/gas mark 8-9, to ensure that it is well sealed and will retains its juices. Reduce the temperature as soon as the meat has browned and baste with its own juices.
- Brush roasts with some form of fat before placing in the oven to cook – use oil and butter, just oil, or goose fat and baste frequently during the early stages of cooking, when the flesh has not yet become caramelised. Don't add salt until mid-way through the cooking process, because salt draws out the juices and prevents the meat from browning.
- When the meat has finished cooking, remove from the oven, cover in aluminium foil and leave to stand for ten minutes before carving. The juices will seep back to the outer layers of the roast and the muscle fibres will relax, improving the tenderness of the meat.

LAMB: marinate a leg of lamb in oil, herbs and crushed garlic, ideally the day before cooking.

Seasoned breadcrumbs

Try coating a leg of lamb before roasting with anchovy butter or brush it with oil and coat in a mixture of breadcrumbs, chopped herbs and coarsely chopped hazelnuts.

■ Lamb chops are fatty enough already, so to prepare, simply brush with oil using a pastry brush, or rub the bottom of the frying pan with kitchen paper soaked in oil.

■ As cooked lamb and mutton fat congeals very quickly, always serve these meats on warm plates.

■ Make moussaka, meat croquettes or stuffed tomatoes with the leftovers from a roast leg of lamb.

BEEF: when cooking beef casserole, the zest of an orange added at the start, will bring out the flavour remarkably well.

■ Decide in advance what type of beef casserole you want to produce. If you want a full-flavoured rich stew, salt after the casserole is cooked; if you prefer your meat more on the juicy side, add the salt at the start; if your aim is a bit of both, salt mid-way through cooking! Similarly, if you start cooking a casserole with cold water, the resulting stock will be full of flavour, but if you start with hot water you'll get flavoursome meat.

■ Simmer slowly, never fast boil, and skim off any impurities that rise to the surface, at regular intervals.

■ A fennel bulb added to the water used for cooking meat will lend a pleasant, aniseed flavour to the stock. If you don't have a fennel bulb to hand, use star anise, instead.

■ If you have any meat stock left over, store it in a container in the freezer; it'll prove invaluable when preparing a last minute risotto.

■ Add colour to stock with a small sachet of onion skins or a concentrate used for colouring and flavouring stews such as a stock cube. The pods of garden peas, dried in the oven, will also work just as well.

■ Skim meat stock, removing any fat with a piece of kitchen paper, folded into a triangle, and repeat several times, until no fat remains on the surface of the stock. An easy way to remove fat from a stew is to cook it the day before and leave to chill. When cold the fat will solidify on the surface, from where it can easily be removed. Combine all the vegetables together in a muslin bag. This makes it easier to fish them out, without damaging them, once the meat has finished cooking.

■ Casserole leftovers can be put to good use for making shepherd's pie. You can also reheat them in a tomato sauce.

The very substance

To prevent bone marrow from escaping during cooking, wrap the bone in leek leaves and secure with string.

Steamed shoulder of lamb

This novel way to cook shoulder of lamb allows the meat to absorb the aroma of spices, herbs, and seasonings, and the meat also retains its succulence.

Serves 6:
■ 3lb 5oz/1.5kg shoulder of lamb
■ handful cooking salt
■ ground pepper
■ 2 tablespoons olive oil
■ 2 cloves garlic crushed
■ 2 teaspoons ground cumin
■ 1 pinch Espelette pepper
■ sprig thyme chopped

Rub the shoulder of lamb with the salt and pepper. Coat with the olive oil and crushed garlic and sprinkle with cumin, Espelette pepper and thyme. Wrap the shoulder in a thin linen cloth, secure and place the meat in a steamer. Bring to the boil and then cook for about 1¼ hours

VEAL: before cooking veal in a frying pan, marinate the day before in the juice of two lemons; the veal will be more tender and flavoursome thanks to this marinade.

■ When sautéing veal, sprinkle with half a glass of beer while cooking. For improved flavour, combine several different cuts of veal.

■ To achieve really tender roast veal, cook in a casserole, rather than in a roasting pan in the oven.

■ Cook blanquette of veal in advance, but don't fold in the egg or cream until the last minute, because they should never reach boiling point.

■ Add two crushed tomatoes, or a spoonful of tomato purée, to osso buco before cooking, and add a strip of blanched lemon zest, three quarters of the way through.

■ Freshly purchased calf's liver should have a thick, smooth, sinew-free and non-grainy appearance. Don't brown veal in a pan because it burns easily. Start cooking the meat slowly in warm oil, for three to five minutes each side. Deglaze the frying pan with sherry vinegar and reduce the resulting sauce over a high heat.

PORK: for much more flavoursome pork, marinate the meat for a few hours in a mixture of lemon juice and oil, before roasting. Flavour with sage, shallots and garlic during cooking.

■ As pork is a fatty meat, it's better to baste it with water rather than oil, during cooking. Loin of pork should be cooked very slowly for about three hours, at 300°F/150°C/gas mark 2-3); the meat will be much more succulent when cooked at this temperature. Roast pork will also be more tasty if you precook it in milk for 15 minutes before roasting.

■ To refresh chilled sausage meat, rinse in cold water, and slit the pack lengthways for easy removal.

■ To prevent meat used for making pâté sticking to your hands, soak them in cold water before kneading the ingredients.

■ Store uncooked ham in a mesh ham cover made of muslin or a loose weave cotton and hang in a cool place. Alternatively wrap in linen and store in a refrigerator compartment. However, the best bit of advice, according to our butcher, is to eat it as quickly as possible. In fact, if you procrastinate it may become too salty and one way to avoid this happening is to rub the ham with pepper or sprinkle with Espelette pepper.

Grilled black pudding

Choose a black pudding with a smooth, blotch-free casing that doesn't stick to the flesh. Prick with a needle to prevent the skin from bursting in the heat and cook very gently under a grill or in a frying pan. To grill, insert wooden skewers crosswise through the pudding to make it easier to turn over.

Salted foie gras

Raw foie gras can be 'cooked' quite simply in rock salt. With this method of preparation, you'll only have to wait for 24 hours before you can sample it.

Serves 10:
- 1 large duck foie gras liver
- 1¾ pt/1 l milk
- 4½ lb/2 kg rock salt
- pepper

Soak the liver in milk for an hour; pat dry with kitchen paper and season with pepper. Wrap in muslin, and place on a bed of rock salt in a deep-sided dish, cover with the remaining salt. Leave in the refrigerator for 24 hours, then remove the salt along with the gauze and wipe the liver. Store in the refrigerator for no longer than six days.

Don't throw away any leftover scraps of ham, as they can be put to good use by adding them to cabbage soup, dried beans and omelettes.

POULTRY AND GAME

■ Don't gut poultry if you have to store it for 48 hours or more before cooking or eating, because the entrails prevent the flesh from oxidising. As with other meats, for best results, poultry should be removed from the refrigerator an hour before cooking.

■ The flesh of fowl will be less fatty if cooked in a casserole. First, brown in a frying pan for five minutes and then discard the fat produced by the meat. Add the neck and the giblets to the casserole to improve the juices, cover and finish cooking.

■ Poultry stuffing should be pre-cooked before cooking inside the bird.

■ If after roasting you intend serving the poultry cold, place the cooked bird on its back so that the juices continue to permeate the roast meat. Never leave a cooked bird to cool down in the refrigerator because it will lose some of its flavour.

■ Use the giblets and the carcass to make stock. Add them to 1¾ pint/1 litre of water containing three carrots, two leeks, an onion and stick of celery. Cook for an hour, then strain. This stock will keep for three days in the refrigerator.

DUCK: is fine roasted if it is young. Stuff with olives that have been blanched to remove some of their salty brine content.

■ Before preparing finely sliced duck breasts, freeze them so that they're easier to slice. Then flavour and garnish with a little tapenade and a light sprinkling of parmesan shavings.

■ Prepare an omelette using fried slices of duck and fried croutons – a delicious traditional recipe from south west France. In spring, sprinkle with green spring garlic.

FOIE GRAS: freshly purchased, uncooked goose or duck foie gras liver should have shiny lobes and range in colour between pink and a pinkish beige.

■ To cut foie gras into perfectly even pieces, dip your knife, at intervals, into very hot water.

■ When preparing foie gras whether part-cooked or tinned, season the lobes with a mixture of salt and ground pepper in a ratio of three parts salt to one part pepper.

Roast breast of duck

Duck breasts are ideal for roasting because they can be cooked in pairs in the oven, just like a joint of meat. Score the fatty skin in a branching pattern for decorative effect. Season the meat with salt and pepper and insert slivers of garlic into the skin. Arrange the duck breasts in pairs, head to toe, and tie together. Cook in a pre-heated oven at 350°F/180°C/gas mark 4 for 20 minutes, if required rare, for longer, if not. Enjoy eating breast of duck with blanched quince (see page 117).

■ Foie gras, eaten at room temperature, is much richer and tastier so remove it from the refrigerator two to three hours before serving.

■ Lend a festive touch to your foie gras by sprinkling it with Szechwan pepper which has been dry-roasted in a frying pan, just before serving.

■ Use leftover, part-cooked foie gras for flavouring poultry stock or pasta, adding it during the final stages of cooking.

HARE: to cook jugged hare, marinate the portions for 12 to 24 hours. Don't add salt to the marinade (see page 36). Drain and wipe the pieces of meat before cooking. Don't throw away the marinade, but strain it and use it to cover the meat during cooking.

RABBIT: a decent rabbit is identified by its blemish-free liver and by its fleshy saddle.

■ If you intend to sauté rabbit in a frying pan, cook it very gently so that it caramelises to a golden brown colour. Add the chopped liver with rosemary during the final stage of cooking.

QUAIL: these small game birds are not cooked that often, and yet they're delicious grilled over a wood fire, nicely browned and juicy. They are also excellent for flavouring stock.

CHICKEN: to cook evenly, chicken should be placed on one side, leg downwards, then turned over on to the leg on the other side, and finally placed breast down for the last stage of cooking.

■ Baste the chicken frequently while cooking with a mixture of oil and a little curry powder, or oil and herbs such as thyme and rosemary, and Espelette pepper. A glass of salted water added to the pan mid-way through cooking moistens the flesh and breaks down the juices.

■ In spring, it's a good idea to stuff your chicken with a bunch of new season garlic.

■ To retain its white colour while cooking, rub the chicken, thoroughly, with the pulp of a lemon. Cook slowly in stock, and check to see whether the chicken is cooked by sticking a fine knitting needle or sharp knife into the thickest part of the flesh – the juices should flow clear, when cooked.

Full-flavoured rabbit

Marinate the rabbit overnight in olive oil, salt, pepper, rosemary, thyme and lemon thyme. The result is a rabbit that is moist and full of flavour.

Succulent guinea fowl

There's so little flesh on guinea fowl, that the meat can have a dry texture if you simply roast it. To make guinea fowl more succulent, place some fromage frais inside the cavity of the bird, or perhaps one or two portions of petit-suisse cream cheese along with some chopped herbs such as tarragon, chervil or parsley. This tip works equally well with chicken. Guinea fowl can also be cooked with vegetables, which have first been trimmed and quick-fried in a little oil.

EGGS
& DAIRY
PRODUCTS

'THEY CAN'T EVEN BOIL AN EGG!' IS THE-OFT QUOTED DESCRIPTION OF SOMEONE WHO DOESN'T KNOW HOW TO COOK. BUT WHAT COULD BE TASTIER THAN A PERFECT FRIED EGG SERVED WITH SOME TOMATO SAUCE, OR A POACHED EGG ON A BED OF CURLY-LEAF SALAD? TO ACHIEVE THIS THE EGG MUST BE EXTREMELY FRESH AND COOKED TO PERFECTION. AS FOR OTHER DAIRY PRODUCTS, THEY'VE LONG BEEN A STAPLE PART OF OUR DIET – RIPE CHEESES, YOGHURTS, DIFFERENT TYPES OF CREAM – ALL HAVE BEEN ADAPTED TO SUIT OUR EVERYDAY TASTES.

Coddled quail's eggs

Serve this original starter with a choice of garnish – diced foie gras, thin strips of truffle, or a selection of herbs.

Serves 4:
- 12 very fresh quail's eggs
- choice of garnish
- 4 teaspoons tapenade or tomato sauce
- buttered ramekins
- salt, pepper

Break three eggs into each ramekin and add your chosen ingredients. Then add a teaspoon of tapenade or tomato sauce to each ramekin. Cover with aluminium foil, set in a bain-marie, and bake in an oven preheated at 300°F/150°C/gas mark 2 for three minutes.

EGGS

■ How can you tell if an egg is fresh? Place the egg in a glass of salt water; if it sits at the bottom of the glass, then it is fresh, if it rises to the top, you'd better not eat it.

■ Spotting the difference between a hard-boiled and a raw egg, when both are stored in the refrigerator, is not always that straightforward. Here's a tip that may help: if you spin the egg, and it spins like a top, then the egg is hard-boiled.

■ Eggs last longer if they're stored with the pointed end facing downwards, which means that the air in the rounded end of the egg is not compressed by the yolk.

■ If you have some egg whites left over from recipes that require only the yolks, don't be afraid to freeze them; egg whites freeze well and won't deteriorate in the freezer. Simply defrost as required, for example, to make beaten egg whites.

■ To separate an egg yolk from the white, crack the egg into a small funnel placed on top of a glass. The yolk will catch in the neck of the funnel, while the white will flow down into the glass. Just make sure that you don't split the yolk when cracking the eggshell!

■ When boiling eggs, if the shell is cracked, wipe the crack with lemon juice before placing the egg in the boiling water. The white will congeal along the crack, sealing it and preventing the contents from escaping.

■ As egg yolk blackens silver, cutlery that has come into contact with egg yolk should be washed immediately after use. Rub egg spoons, or utensils used with eggs, with a potato cut in half.

■ To remove egg stains, first scrape off the excess, then soak the fabric in a solution of cold water and salt.

HARD-BOILED EGGS: cooking the perfect hard-boiled egg is not as easy as it seems when the aim is to achieve a white that is smooth and not rubbery, and a yolk that's cooked to perfection

The flavour of truffle

Store some eggs, for a few days, in a preserving jar containing a fresh truffle and topped up with rice. Both the eggs and the rice will be infused with the wonderful aroma of truffle.

with no green tinges round the edge. Place the egg in boiling water and time it for exactly ten minutes, simmering throughout and rolling it over gently, at intervals, to keep the yolk positioned in the centre. Remove the egg from the water and immediately immerse it in a bowl of cold water to make it easier to shell.

POACHED EGGS: poaching is a rather delicate operation. Heat the water to which a little lemon juice or vinegar has been added. Crack the egg into a bowl, then lower the bowl so the egg is level with the simmering water and slide it in, all in one go. Remove from the heat, cover the pan and leave to stand for four minutes. Take out the egg using a slotted spoon, draining and trimming any strands of white with kitchen scissors, so that the poached egg looks presentable. Serve with spinach purée or watercress.

SCRAMBLED EGGS: are prepared over a very gentle heat, using a heavy-based saucepan and a bain-marie. If the eggs start cooking too quickly, add a beaten egg yolk. To stop the cooking process, fold in some crème fraîche – a teaspoon per egg. Scrambled eggs that aren't to be served immediately should be kept on a plate set on top of a saucepan containing hot water.

SOFT-BOILED EGGS: remove the egg from the refrigerator at least two hours before cooking to avoid the cold shell cracking when placed in hot water. Next, place the egg in boiling water and cook for exactly three minutes and three seconds. Alternatively, place the egg in cold water and bring to the boil, leave for a few seconds and remove from the heat.

OMELETTE: to make the perfect omelette you'll need to equip yourself with a good frying pan with a heavy base. Rub the bowl into which the eggs will be broken, with garlic. Never cook more than six eggs at a time – this will serve two or three people. For a more flavoursome omelette, lightly beat the egg whites and yolks separately. Combine them, adding a little crème fraîche or milk, or for a lighter result two tablespoons of water. Pour the mixture into a very hot frying pan. Season the omelette with chopped herbs such as chervil, parsley or chives.

■ Make individual omelettes using just two eggs per person and cook on one side only (don't turn or fold the omelette) and garnish with flowers, herbs, or wafer-thin rounds of chorizo sausage.

Fried eggs

It's better to fry eggs in a blend of oil and butter; butter alone tends to blacken the eggs if used at too high a temperature. A drop of vinegar added to the frying pan will help cook the whites and also help you slide the cooked eggs out of the pan more easily. If possible use a wooden spatula, as metal tends to stick to eggs.

Eggs mimosa

Eggs mimosa has recently enjoyed a revival in popularity, and is a recipe that's inevitably savoured with a tinge of nostalgia.

Serves 6:
- 6 hard-boiled eggs
- 12 teaspoons mayonnaise
- 12 chervil leaves
- salt, pepper

Halve the eggs, lengthways, and remove the yolks; set one yolk aside and mash the remaining yolks with a fork. Fold mayonnaise into the mashed yolks and use the mixture to fill the halved egg whites. Roughly chop the remaining egg yolk and sprinkle over the other eggs, garnishing each half with a chervil leaf.

■ Make a layered omelette cake by placing several different flavoured omelettes on top of each other. Cut slices through the layers as you would through a cake.

■ Don't forget that sweet omelettes, using apples or apricots, for example, make delicious desserts.

DAIRY PRODUCTS

BUTTER: store in the refrigerator wrapped in a damp tea towel.

■ To harden butter, immerse in water containing ice cubes. Conversely, if you want to soften butter, pop it in the microwave for a few seconds, or grate using a coarse grater.

■ If you're out of butter, try making your own; pour ⅓ pt/20 cl of thick crème fraîche into a blender bowl and mix for at least five minutes. Strain, cream the mixture and rinse the butter produced in fresh water.

■ To restore the freshness of rancid butter, soak in a salad bowl full of iced water containing bicarbonate of soda then mix briskly. The bicarbonate destroys the germs responsible for fermentation and eliminates its rancid taste. Another trick is to insert a piece of raw carrot into the rancid butter; it will absorb the unpleasant smell.

■ Clarified butter doesn't burn and is therefore highly prized for all types of cooking, especially for dishes cooked at a high temperature, such as sautéed potatoes. It is also useful for preparing sauces because it doesn't burn and therefore blacken.

■ To make clarified butter, melt some butter in a saucepan, over a low heat; then set aside until the whey sinks to the bottom and the froth rises to the surface. Remove as much of the froth as possible using a skimmer, and filter off the rest by pouring gently through a fine sieve into a jar, ensuring throughout that the whey remains at the bottom of the saucepan. Clarified butter prepared in this way will keep for up to a month in the refrigerator.

■ Add a floral touch to your butter by blending it with the petals of edible flowers such as marigolds, violets, nasturtiums or borage.

MILK: to prevent milk boiling over, place an inverted saucer in the bottom of the pan. This trick works equally well when making jam.

■ To avoid milk sticking to the bottom of a saucepan, rinse the pan out with cold water, before adding the milk.

Glue made from milk

If you run out of glue for sticking labels on bottles or jam jars, brush them with milk and they'll stick perfectly.

Flavoured butters

Flavour small pats of butter with different flavours – shallots, garlic, anchovy, Roquefort cheese, parsley, thyme, lemon or truffle – and then select the butter that is most appropriate for your menu, on a daily basis. Flavoured butters can also be spread on toasted bread and enjoyed with aperitifs.

■ Although not particularly health giving, condensed milk (both sweetened and unsweetened) has fond memories for many of us! Condensed milk is also the base ingredient for a simple yet delicious recipe for milk jam: place a can of sweetened condensed milk in a bain-marie and cook for two hours. Allow the can to cool before opening it; then taste with a teaspoon...

FROMAGE BLANC: a soft white cheese similar to thick yoghurt. Always strain un-whipped fromage blanc through a sieve before folding into the remaining ingredients.

■ For a quick and easy fresh dessert, simply add fromage blanc to a soft fruit coulis. For a savoury variation, use fromage blanc seasoned with spices or herbs such as parsley, chervil, tarragon or shallots, then add a dash of olive oil and vinegar, a pinch of salt and a twist of the pepper mill and serve as a starter.

■ Replace half the fat content of a cake or gateau with fromage blanc (or yoghurt); this makes it easier on the digestion.

YOGHURT: if you don't have a set of scales to hand, use a yoghurt pot instead to measure the ingredients for cakes, puddings and confectionery, bearing in mind that a 4½ oz/125g yoghurt pot will hold 4½ oz/125g sugar, and 3 oz/85 g flour.

■ Don't throw away yoghurt that is date-expired; instead spread it on the outside of earthenware garden pots to encourage a patina of age.

CHEESE: store cheese in its original wrapping paper, in either a cool place or, if there's no alternative, in the vegetable basket of your refrigerator. Cheese stored in a refrigerator tends to lose some of its mellowness and flavour.

■ Cheeses freeze well; but make sure that they are eaten within three months of freezing.

■ Dried out cheese can be resurrected by wrapping it in a tea towel that has been soaked in a bowl of water containing rock salt. Treated in this way cheese will regain its moisture within a few hours.

■ Gruyère stored under a cheese dome will not dry out as quickly if you place a couple of sugar lumps alongside the piece of cheese. If you slip two or three sprigs of thyme under the cheese dome, it will minimise the pungency of fully ripened cheeses.

■ Don't throw away leftover pieces of cheese; grate them instead and use in vegetable gratins or savoury tarts.

■ Grated cheese won't stick together if you spread it on a piece of bread, which absorbs the moisture.

Aperitif croquettes

Season fresh goat's cheese by rolling it in spices or seasonings – turmeric, Espelette pepper, chopped shallots, thyme or ground hazelnuts – and serve with aperitifs.

Goat's cheese in oil

If your goat's cheese is too dry, marinate it in olive oil with a few sprigs of thyme and rosemary; the cheese will stay perfectly fresh in this marinade for several weeks.

PASTA, RICE & CEREALS

IGNORED BY TOP CHEFS FOR MANY YEARS, TODAY PASTA, RICE AND CEREALS ARE ON EVERYONE'S MENU – THEIR HEALTH-GIVING PROPERTIES BEING, QUITE SIMPLY, GOOD FOR YOU! DO YOU KNOW ANYONE WHO DOESN'T LIKE PASTA, OR SOMEONE WHO DOESN'T APPRECIATE A DELICIOUS RISOTTO? BUT, AS WITH ALL DISHES THAT APPEAR STRAIGHTFORWARD, CERTAIN RULES MUST BE FOLLOWED IF THEY'RE TO TURN OUT SUCCESSFULLY. AND, AS WITH OTHER TYPES OF CEREAL, THEY REQUIRE A COOK WHO IS WILLING TO EXPLORE THEIR POSSIBILITIES AND LEARN HOW TO COOK THEM.

PASTA

Pasta omelette

Make a pasta omelette with spaghetti, linguini or large vermicelli leftovers; mix with beaten egg and cook as you would an omelette. Equally tasty hot or cold, this dish is perfect for picnics.

■ According to the rules, the art of cooking pasta so that it doesn't stick together demands a big enough pan for the water to boil freely, a large volume of water (1¾ pt/1 litre of water per 3½ oz/100 g of pasta), and that you do not add salt until the pasta has reached boiling point.

■ If you stick to these guidelines, there is absolutely no need to add oil to the water. However, there is one exception; a little oil should be added to the water used for cooking lasagne so that the sheets don't stick together.

■ As soon as pasta has been plunged into boiling water, cover the pan with a lid so that it returns to boiling point as quickly as possible. When it has returned to the boil, remove the lid and stir the pasta with a fork.

■ Pasta should be cooked *al dente*, in other words, a texture that's both soft and firm. When the pasta is just cooked, remove from the heat and pour a glass of cold water into the pan to stop it from continuing to cook. Wait 30 seconds before draining, and, above all, don't rinse under running water, which will make it lose flavour and nutrients.

■ Save some of the water used for cooking for thinning the sauce, if necessary.

■ For an alternative cooking method, once the pasta has been added to the boiling water in the saucepan and reaches simmering point once again, switch off the gas, cover the pan with a large cloth folded in four and place the lid on top. The pasta continues cooking, unattended. After ten minutes, the pasta should be perfectly cooked. Drain and serve.

■ Pour cooked pasta and the cooking water into a sieve placed on top of a large salad bowl, to reheat.

■ To ensure a balanced combination of pasta and sauce, stir, then stir again until the sauce has thoroughly penetrated the pasta: this procedure is particularly important when using pasta tubes such as penne and rigatoni.

The 10, 100, 1000 rule

A useful mnemonic for successful pasta is to stick to the 10, 100, 1000 rule – 10 g of salt, 100 g of pasta, 1,000 g (1 litre) of water.

■ For pasta that will not be eaten immediately, drain, put in a bowl and add a knob of butter or olive oil, ready for reheating by placing on top of a saucepan of boiling water.

■ Use a slotted spoon to remove the more delicate types of pasta such as filled pasta, or lasagne from the water, or gnocchi when it resurfaces in the pan.

DRIED PASTA: allow 2 oz/60 g of dried pasta per person, if serving as an accompaniment and 3½ oz/100 g for a main dish.

■ Small pasta shapes are more suitable for salads such as orechiette and melon ball salad, small penne salad with a mild pepper coulis, farfalle pasta salad with fresh tomatoes.

■ Macaroni gratin is better if you leave the pasta to swell in a meat stock before making into a gratin. Pour a ladle of the cooked stock into the gratin dish.

■ Spaghetti is often served with mussels or a mussel sauce. For a change, serve it with different shellfish or clams.

■ For a lighter version of spaghetti carbonara substitute the crème fraîche and butter with soy sauce and olive oil. Thin the beaten egg mixture with a few spoons of the water used for cooking the pasta to achieve a creamy mixture.

FRESH PASTA: when serving pasta as a main dish, allow 4¼ oz/120 g of fresh pasta per person.

■ Note that fresh pasta made with eggs cooks faster than dried pasta and needs only about one to two minutes for most varieties, and even less for certain types such as angel hair pasta.

■ It's important to cook fresh pasta just before serving, when your guests are already seated at the table, so that when it's ready, all that remains is to add the sauce and serve.

■ Serve plain fresh pasta, to accompany stews or beef casserole.

■ Ravioli retains the right texture if you don't cook it for longer than a minute, and if it isn't boiled too briskly. Don't drain completely so that the sauce blends better with the ravioli.

QUICK AND EASY SAUCES: cook light and digestible pasta dishes by adding the juice and grated rind of a lemon, some fine quality olive oil, salt and pepper to linguini or large penne pasta.

■ Immediately before serving, sprinkle the pasta with shavings of parmesan and garnish with flat-leaved parsley.

Vegetable tagliatelli

Slice unpeeled courgettes using a mandolin slicer, cook and add to tagliatelle enriched with crème fraîche coloured with saffron.

Fresh egg pasta

Here is the basic recipe for fresh homemade pasta. Cut the pasta into the shape required by the recipe to make noodles, lasagne, ravioli, etc.

To make 1 lb 2 oz/500g of pasta:
■ 10½ oz/300 g flour (plus some extra flour for dusting the work surface)
■ 3 eggs
■ pinch salt

Arrange the flour in a dome on the work surface, make a well in the centre, break the eggs into it and add the salt. Mix the flour into the eggs by hand, and knead the pasta for 10 to 15 minutes until the dough becomes pliable and elastic. Roll to form a ball, wrap in cling film and leave to prove for 30 minutes. Dust the work surface with flour and knead the pasta, stretching and turning several times, a quarter of a turn at a time, until the pasta is ⅛ in/2–3 mm thick.

■ Season small dried pastas, like penne or orechiette, with avocado, rocket leaves, olive oil, salt, pepper and parmesan.

■ Serve hollow-style pastas, such as large penne or rigatoni, with a pepper-based coulis made from a jar of preserved red peppers mixed with a little crème frâiche, a pinch of salt and pepper and a drop of olive oil.

■ Blend three or four anchovies in oil, a clove of garlic and a teaspoon of capers, with some olive oil and use it to sprinkle over penne or farfalle pasta.

Milanese risotto

This very simple risotto is extremely tasty — if you follow our cooking instructions to the letter!

Serves 6:
■ 1 carrot chopped
■ 1 onion chopped
■ 1 stick celery chopped
■ 2 tablespoons olive oil
■ 1 lb 2 oz/500 g carnaroli or arborio short grain Italian rice
■ ⅓ pt/20 cl dry white wine
■ 2½ pt/1.5 l poultry stock
■ 2 oz/60 g butter
■ 1¾ oz/50 g grated parmesan
■ salt, pepper

In a high-sided frying pan, sweat the chopped vegetables in a small amount of olive oil, without browning, then add the rice and stir until the mixture becomes translucent. Pour in the white wine and simmer until it is absorbed. Pour in the stock, cover and cook gently for 15 to 20 minutes. Add the butter, stir, sprinkle with the parmesan and mix briskly to combine all the ingredients, thoroughly. Season with salt and pepper.

RICE

■ Allow about 1 oz/25-30 g of rice per person for a starter, 2-2½ oz/60-70 g for a main dish and 1½ oz/40 g for dessert.

■ As there are many different varieties of rice, always use the type of rice specified in the recipe. Opt for short grain rice, such as rice from the Camargue, for desserts like rice pudding and for making paella. Coarse, short grain rice like arborio or carnaroli is recommended for making risottos.

■ Long grain, almond-flavoured jasmine rice and basmati rice are best served plain in salads or as an accompaniment for poultry dishes. Basmati rice is also used in pilau recipes.

■ Red rice goes well with vegetables and lentils in vegetarian dishes.

■ Wild rice is often used in combination with white rice, or on its own as an accompaniment for game.

■ If your rice is overcooked or lacking in flavour, mix in a beaten egg and grated parmesan and leave in the oven until golden brown.

■ For very white-coloured rice, add the juice of half a lemon to the cooking water; for extra fragrance, add a bay leaf broken in half.

■ To colour rice, mix a pinch of saffron, curry powder or turmeric with the cooking water.

■ Use ground rice for baking — it's gluten-free and makes lighter cakes and pastries.

■ Never rinse rice used for making risottos as washing destroys the starch content which is the vital ingredient of a fine risotto.

■ Coat risotto rice grains in fat, either butter or oil, and cook for a minute, no more. This prevents the rice from boiling until the grains split, destroying their precious starch content.

It never sticks!

Stir rice once only, when you start the cooking process, because if you stir it too often the starch is released which will make it sticky. If this does happen, rinse in cold water.

■ To make a successful risotto, the stock must be kept at a high temperature so that it's hot when it permeates the rice, thus avoiding the need to halt or unnecessarily extend the cooking process.

■ Use seasonally available produce to create variations on the basic risotto recipe. Garden peas and asparagus in spring, tomatoes, shellfish and herbs in the summer, cep and chanterelle mushrooms in the autumn and foie gras and truffles during the winter.

■ Don't waste leftover risotto; simply add a beaten egg, some grated parmesan, parsley and dried breadcrumbs to the cold rice and, using the palms of your hands, shape into small balls, and deep fry until golden brown. These are best eaten piping hot!

CEREALS

SEMOLINA: for couscous use medium-ground semolina grains. Heat in a couscous maker with a large knob of butter and two tablespoons of olive oil; rubbing the ingredients with your hands.

■ To make tastier polenta, using ground maize semolina, cook it in meat stock. The longer it cooks, the better.

QUINOA: cook quinoa grains for 15 to 20 minutes in twice its volume of cold, salted water. When cooked, cover the pan and allow the grains to expand for two minutes. You can eat quinoa with a salad adding a Provençal basil and garlic sauce, in an aubergine gratin with a drizzle of olive oil, or as an accompaniment for a roast or poultry dish.

BULGAR WHEAT: for greater flavour, cook in an infusion of aromatic herbs including bay, thyme or rosemary, or in the liquid from a vegetable stock cube.

■ Bulgar wheat can be used instead of semolina grains for making couscous or tabbouleh.

SPELT: a nutty flavoured type of wheat which cooks in exactly the same way as risotto rice, using the same ingredients. It has a unique and delicious flavour and is ideal as an accompaniment for roast poultry.

A sprinkling of semolina

To avoid lumps forming, always sprinkle semolina grains from a height into a pan containing dairy products and stock.

Vegetarian stuffed tomatoes

In recipes for stuffed tomatoes, aubergines or courgettes, replace the meat in the stuffing with quinoa.

Serves 6:
- 6 large tomatoes
- 1 onion chopped
- 2 button mushrooms, chopped
- 2 tablespoons olive oil
- 5¼ oz/150 g quinoa
- salt, pepper
- chopped parsley, chives and coriander
- 1 tablespoon toasted sesame seeds

Carefully scoop out the tomato centres and chop up the flesh. Lightly brown this tomato pulp in a frying pan with a little olive oil, the onion and the mushrooms. Cook the hollowed out tomatoes in the oven for 20 minutes at 325°F/170°C/gas mark 3. Meanwhile, cook the quinoa in twice its volume of cold, salted water for 15 minutes, then drain. Mix with the cooked tomato, mushrooms and onion and season with salt and pepper. Add the chopped herbs, along with the toasted sesame seeds and use this mixture to stuff the tomatoes.

FRESH & DRIED FRUITS, CONSERVES & JAMS

THE OLD ADAGE SAYS, 'APPLES LAST LONGER PLACED UPSIDE DOWN, WHEREAS PEARS KEEP BETTER THE RIGHT WAY UP'. IN THE PAST FRUIT USED TO BE STORED ON FRUIT RACKS OR SPREAD OUT ON SHEETS OF NEWSPAPER TO REDUCE THE EFFECTS OF HUMIDITY. EVERY FAMILY WOULD MAKE THEIR OWN JAMS AND FRUIT PRESERVES, OR SIMPLY USE THE FRUIT TO PRODUCE WINE TO OFFER GUESTS AS A WELCOMING GESTURE. TODAY, WE ARE TRYING TO RECAPTURE THOSE REAL FRUIT FLAVOURS OF YEARS GONE BY, FLAVOURS WHICH SOMEHOW SEEM TO BE SADLY LACKING IN MANY MODERN VARIETIES.

FRESH FRUIT

PINEAPPLES: should not be stored in a refrigerator as they will not ripen properly under these conditions. Choose a cool and humid place, instead.

■ Glaze slices of fresh pineapple with butter and sugar, and drizzle generously with rum to make a very fine dessert.

APRICOTS: stock up on apricots when they are just ripe and store them in the freezer, then use the frozen fruit in the winter months to make compotes and tarts.

■ For an apricot tart, put the halves skin side down on the pastry so that it doesn't become soggy.

BANANAS: deteriorate in the refrigerator because the cold makes them turn black.

■ Don't peel bananas too far in advance, as their flesh is likely to oxidise. If, for whatever reason, you need to prepare bananas beforehand, sprinkle them with lemon juice.

■ Slit the entire banana skin, lengthwise, and cook the fruit in the oven at 375°F/190°C/gas mark 5, for 10 to 15 minutes. Remove the skin, dredge the banana with vanilla sugar, and serve warm.

FIGS: have skins that are too delicate to be washed, so make do with wiping them on paper kitchen towel.

■ Figs are ideal for freezing, but make sure that you arrange them carefully, side by side, in a container.

■ Baked, preserved figs, with or without their leaves, make superb accompaniments for poultry dishes, as well as for various foie gras recipes.

PEACHES: Sprinkle a little freshly ground Szechwan pepper or ground coriander over peach slices which have been browned in butter and sugar in a frying pan. This will improve their flavour.

Criss-cross figs

To make an attractive fig dish, remove their stalks and cut a criss-cross into the top of each fig. Drizzle with honey, sprinkle with grated lemon rind and roast in the oven.

Peach skins

Peach skins peel more easily if they are poached first for a few minutes in boiling water before steeping in cold water. A steamer works just as well; simply steam for five minutes.

MANGOES: you can't tell how ripe the fruit is from the colour of its skin. It's only by feeling a mango that you can gauge whether it's sufficiently ripe – it needs to be pliable but not too soft.

■ Mangoes can be used to replace the traditional melon accompaniment for cooked ham.

■ Cut a peeled mango into thin slices with a very sharp knife, slicing from top to bottom. As a starter, one mango is sufficient to serve four people.

■ Cut mangoes into 1½ in/4 cm cubes, brown in a little butter in a frying pan, and serve as an accompaniment for roast guinea fowl, roast veal or a pork roast.

MELONS: if you have a melon that's past its best, use it for making a salad rather than eating it on its own. Scoop melon balls out of the flesh using a melon ball scoop, season with a drop of olive oil and a white wine vinegar such as Banyuls vinegar, then garnish with small, black olives and shavings of parmesan.

PEARS: once peeled, pears oxidise and brown quickly. To counter this effect, sprinkle peeled pears with lemon juice.

■ If cooking pears whole, peel them but leave the stalks attached for a more attractive presentation.

■ To intensify the colour of pears cooked in red wine, add four tablespoons of cassis liqueur to the cooking liquid. If you want to thicken the syrup, add a teaspoonful of cornflour, mix thoroughly and boil briskly for a few seconds.

APPLES: are best stored away from other fruits because they release ethylene, a gas that accelerates the ripening process.

■ Fruit compotes made from slightly acidic apples taste delicious with just a knob of butter, a star anise and a sachet of vanilla sugar added.

QUINCES: this fruit can be slightly bitter or hard and it requires rubbing with half a lemon to avoid oxidation and blanching for 15 minutes before adding to a recipe.

■ Divide a quince in two, sprinkle with sugar and roast in the oven for an hour. Roast duck breasts, fried foie gras, game and pork make perfect partners for this side dish.

PLUMS: if you find plums still with bloom on their skins, purchase immediately because it is an indication of their freshness.

A fine melon

When buying a melon, pick it up and feel the weight of it in your hands. It needs to be heavy and its smell will offer a hint as to whether the melon is past its best, ripe or sweet. If the short stalk is cracked, it's a fair indication that the fruit is ripe. However, always try the melon before serving to your guests!

Mango chutney

Enjoy this chutney with part-cooked foie gras. It will keep for several months in the refrigerator.

Serves 4:
■ 2 shallots, chopped
■ butter (for sweating shallots)
■ 1 large mango, diced
■ curry powder
■ 10½ oz/300 g brown sugar
■ ¼ pt/15 cl sherry vinegar

Sweat the chopped shallots in a little butter and sprinkle with curry powder and add the diced mango. Mix the sugar with the vinegar and pour over the ingredients in the pan. Simmer over a low heat until all the liquid has evaporated. Keep in sterilised jars in the fridge.

■ Before baking large plums in the oven, coat in egg white and granulated sugar. Cook for 15 minutes in a preheated oven at 350°F/180°C/gas mark 4.

GRAPES: blanching grapes in hot water for a few seconds makes them easier to peel.

■ Freeze grapes and use as ice cubes to serve with colourless spirit drinks like rum, vodka or gin.

■ Grapes keep well in the vegetable compartment of the refrigerator – just remember to remove an hour before eating.

SOFT FRUITS

■ These small, delicate fruits should be eaten as soon as possible, and should never be left piled up in their punnets.

■ If you want to freeze these fruits, don't freeze them in bulk, in large bags. Freeze them laid out on a tray, coated in sugar if you prefer, before placing in a freezer pack.

■ A coulis of soft fruits is far superior if you coat the fruit with icing sugar instead of caster sugar.

■ Take care not to let red berry stains dry out. Rub them with a rag soaked in lemon juice and rinse in cold water.

CHERRIES: should be bought in small quantities, so that you can savour them while they're still firm and juicy.

■ Put a cherry in each section of an ice cube tray, fill up with water and freeze: the cherry ice cubes will be much appreciated by cocktail aficionados.

■ Munching fresh cherries is such a delightful experience that it is easy to overlook the fact that cherries cooked for five minutes in a frying pan with a little butter and a sprinkling of sugar make an excellent dessert.

■ Dry some cherry stalks and add to your infusions: they have a diuretic effect.

STRAWBERRIES: a strawberry fruit salad is more fragrant and attractive if you sprinkle it with vanilla sugar and add lemon juice which enhances the flavour and livens up the colour. Add the sugar immediately before serving, as this helps the fruits hold their shape.

■ A drop of balsamic vinegar and a twist of the pepper mill also brings out the flavour of strawberries and cherries, sautéed in butter in a frying pan.

A garland of apples

Dried apples are prepared by placing slices of apple in the oven to dry out at 300°F/150°C/gas mark 2 for about four hours. Thread the pieces of apple on a piece of string and continue drying in the open air.

Harmonious co-existence

Quince added to a dish of stewed apples gives the latter character and substance. If you store both fruits together, the quince fragrance will permeate the apples.

■ The unwaxed leaf of a lemon tree can improve the presentation of a dish, while at the same time adding a hint of lemon flavour to a sauce.

■ Thanks to its antioxidant properties, lemon juice can be used to prevent certain fruits and vegetables from blackening.

■ Lemons also possess antiseptic properties: if you have a sore throat, drink hot lemon juice with a little added honey. Don't heat the lemon juice; simply pour it into a cup of boiling water.

■ Finally, lemons are great for removing difficult stains and rust marks.

ORANGES: To save time, remove the zest of an orange with a paring knife, leaving behind the excessively bitter white pith, grind in a blender and keep in a jar in the refrigerator. This provides a week's supply of ready to use orange zest.

■ To flavour a tart or cake mixture, add some grated orange or lemon peel.

■ Dry orange skins for use in making pot-pourri. Hang it up in the kitchen or place on top of a radiator to sweeten the atmosphere.

■ Make your own pot-pourri sachets yourself, by placing herbs such as rosemary, camomile and eucalyptus, spices like cloves and cinnamon sticks, together with dried orange peel and bits of bark, on a square piece of muslin. Add a few drops of essential oils – lavender or verbena – then lift the four corners of the muslin, fasten together and place the sachets on the shelves of your wardrobe.

GRAPEFRUIT: the skin of this fruit sticks to its flesh, which makes it difficult to peel. To overcome this problem, grapefruit should be put in the refrigerator for two hours beforehand, which dries the white flesh, thus enabling you to peel the grapefruit easily.

KUMQUATS: to soften the skins of kumquats before preserving, or adding to a fruit salad, immerse the fruit in boiling water, cook for five minutes, then cool.

■ To prepare a delicious orange and kumquat salad, halve some kumquats and cook in a syrup made from 3 oz/80 g of sugar and ½ pt/25 cl of water. Add the kumquats to the orange salad and sweeten with the syrup.

Preserved lemon

To make your own preserved lemon, select lemons with thin skins, small Moroccan beldi lemons, if available, are ideal.

For a 4½ lb/2 kg preserving jar:
■ 2¼ lb/1 kg unwaxed beldi lemons (or another variety of small, thin-skinned lemons)
■ 4 tablespoons rock salt
■ 1¾ pt/1 l water

Cut a deep cross shape into each lemon, fill the slits with rock salt and place the lemons in a preserving jar. Cover with water, then leave to steep for two months. Preserved lemon can be used in small quantities to flavour tagine dishes, but due its powerful flavour, it should only be added 20 minutes before the tagine has finished cooking.

Lemon zest

Before removing the zests of waxed citrus fruits, scrub the skins in hot water to remove the wax coating.

JAMS

■ Choose fruits that are at their peak of ripeness for making jam. Ripe fruits offer both flavour and pectin, a natural gelling agent; over-ripe fruit contains no pectin and unripe fruit has no flavour.

■ Keep the stones from plums, cherries and apricots; crack open, wrap them in muslin and cook with the fruit to add a very pleasant almond flavour.

■ You can quite happily use the leftovers from several different types of fruit to make jam, provided, of course, that the fruit isn't damaged.

■ A knob of butter helps to reduce the froth produced when boiling fruit.

■ Jam making can be a less tedious task if you cook the fruit in several small batches, at the same time, and just put the cooking process on hold if you have to go out. You will know that jam is ready for bottling when a few drops placed on a cold plate that has been chilling for an hour in the refrigerator, set instantly.

■ Bottle jam while it's still hot, screw on the lids and invert the jars immediately to create a vacuum, thus ensuring that the jam is well preserved.

■ If you don't have any screw-top lids for your jam jars, cover the jam with round pieces of greaseproof paper soaked in brandy and cover the jars with cellophane circles, secured with elastic bands.

■ If, when you open a pot of jam, you find that the surface has become mouldy, simply remove the mouldy bits as the rest will be perfectly edible, and won't present a health risk. Keep the opened pot of jam in the refrigerator.

DRIED FRUITS, CRYSTALLISED FRUITS AND PRESERVED FRUITS

■ To re-hydrate dried fruits for use in baking, leave to swell in water, tea or alcohol. If the dried fruit is to be used for enriching a sauce, you could soak it in wine with added spices.

■ If you're pressed for time, you can plump up dried fruit in a steamer for two minutes. This tip also applies to preserved fruits that may be slightly over-dry.

■ When preserving fruits in brandy, they should be boiled first and their skins pricked to enable the flesh to absorb the alcohol.

Cold jelly

Prepare a redcurrant jelly without cooking it – a cold jelly. Weigh the fruit and add the same weight in sugar and steep them overnight. Pour the mixture through a sieve, drain off the syrup and pour into jars, which should be left open, exposed to the air, until the liquid sets as a jelly. Screw on the lids and store in the refrigerator.

Non-stick crystallised fruits!

When cutting up crystallised fruits, dip the blade of your knife in hot water to prevent the fruits from sticking to your knife.

PRUNES AND DRIED APRICOTS: choose organically produced apricots and prunes. The apricots will have a brownish appearance. (The usual orange colour is produced by treating the fruit with sulphur dioxide.)

SWEET CHESTNUTS: cut notches in the skins of sweet chestnuts before placing in boiling water. Add a fig leaf to aid the cooking process and cook for 30 minutes.

HAZELNUTS: to peel hazelnuts more easily, bake in the oven for five minutes at 350°F/180°C/gas mark 4. Alternatively, you could plunge the hazelnuts in boiling water and remove when the water comes back to the boil (the same applies to almonds).
■ Give whipped cream a special taste by adding a few cracked hazelnuts.

WALNUTS: it's easy to remove walnut kernels from their shells without breaking them – simply soak the walnuts in sugared water for a few hours before cracking them open.
■ Dried walnuts can taste like fresh walnuts if you steep them in milk for two hours.
■ Make your own walnut stain for staining wood using unripe walnuts. Crush the walnuts, add to boiling water and cook for an hour, then drain.
■ To revive clothes made of black cotton, add two glasses of a solution made from walnut leaves to the final rinse, soaking for 30 minutes.

Prunes in brandy

To prepare dried prunes in brandy, first soak in tea for 12 hours and then pour into a preserving jar and cover with brandy. Flavour with a cinnamon stick and a vanilla pod, halved lengthwise, and leave to steep for at least a month.

Walnut wine

In the past, every French family would make their own walnut wine to serve as a warming welcome to guests or as a drink to aid digestion.

Makes 1¾ pt/1 l:
■ 11 walnut leaves
■ 11 unripe walnuts
■ ⅓ pt/20 cl brandy
■ 2¼ lb/1 kg sugar
■ 3½ pt/2 l red wine

Crush the walnut leaves and walnuts with a hammer or stone and then steep in brandy for 24 hours. Strain, retaining the brandy, and add the leaves and the walnuts to the wine and leave to steep for three days. Strain, add the sugar and the brandy to the strained wine and store in corked bottles in a cool place for two months before tasting.

BREAD, PASTRIES & DESSERTS

BAKING DEMANDS CULINARY SKILL. EVERY COOK HAS, AT ONE TIME OR ANOTHER, HAD PROBLEMS WITH CAKES THAT WON'T RISE, CHOCOLATE THAT IS OVER-COOKED, PASTRY THAT IS UNMANAGEABLE AND DISASTERS LIKE CREAM OOZING EVERYWHERE! SOMETIMES IT IS JUST A MATTER OF ADDING A PINCH OF BICARBONATE OF SODA TO THE DOUGH AND BAKING WITH A LIGHTER TOUCH. GOLDEN RULES EXIST THAT CAN GET US OUT OF SUCH TIGHT SPOTS AND ALLOW US TO BAKE A SUCCESSFUL CAKE, VARY THE FLAVOURS AND PERFECT THE DECORATION OF A DESSERT, WITH PERFECT EASE.

BREAD

- To produce quality breadcrumbs, dry some bread in the oven, place in a tea towel folded in half and crush the bread with a rolling pin. Alternatively, crush melba toast or grate bread crusts or frozen bread using a general-purpose grater.
- Garnish soup or broth with a few small pieces of bread, with the crusts removed, and dried in the oven. To prepare, dice a thick slice of slightly stale bread, with the crusts removed, and dry out in a pre-heated oven at 225°F/110°C/gas mark ¼. Store in a hermetically sealed container.
- To make successful French toast, it is important to drain the slices thoroughly after cooking and not to let the butter blacken.
- Spread olive tapenade or flavoured butter (see page 96) on leftover thin slices of baguette and use as bread soldiers for dipping in soft-boiled eggs.

BAKING

FLOUR: there are several different types of wheat flour. Soft flour, either plain or self-raising, is used for general baking purposes, and strong flour is used for bread making. Flour should always be stored in a cool, dark place.

- Rye and chestnut flour do not rise as much as wheat flour. If you use the former, add a pinch of bicarbonate of soda or a teaspoon of brewer's yeast to the mixture.
- For lighter results when baking cakes, replace a third of the flour with cornflour.

TART PASTRY: once made, seal in cling-film to prevent the pastry from drying out and leave to stand for at least an hour in the refrigerator. You can prepare pastry in bulk for several tarts, rolling the pastry that's not for immediate use into a ball, and freeze. To reuse simply defrost the ball of pastry at room temperature.

More sugar in honey

This natural preservative boosts the richness of cakes. If you use honey instead of sugar, you'll need to use less of it because honey's already sweet enough! In fact, 3½ oz/100 g of honey has the same sweetening effect as 5¼ oz/150 g of sugar.

Fresh, crusty bread

To keep bread fresh, wrap it in a linen cloth with half an apple. To restore crustiness to yesterday's bread, moisten the crust slightly and warm the loaf in the oven.

- To prevent pastry cases from becoming soggy from the filling, glaze the base first with unbeaten egg white or sprinkle with wheat semolina, before adding the filling.
- It's easier to rub butter into flour when it's cut up into small pieces. Leave the butter in the refrigerator until you're ready to make pastry, then grate with a coarse grater.
- Nothing could be easier than giving a piecrust, a pastie crust, or the rim of a tart an attractive golden colour: simply brush on a glaze made with egg yolk or milk, using a pastry brush, before cooking.
- Baking blind involves baking an empty pastry case. Cover the base in greaseproof paper and hold in place with dried beans or ceramic baking beans. Bake for 15 minutes, remove the beans and paper and then bake for a further five minutes.

Shortcrust pastry: handle as little as possible, otherwise the pastry becomes too stretchy. If the butter is too hard, grate using a coarse grater. The water added to bind the flour and butter mixture should be ice cold. If you're adding eggs to the pastry ingredients, only use the yolks because the whites will make your pastry tough.

Puff pastry: is easier to cut with scissors than with a knife, as they don't crush the layers of pastry.

Pastry for sealing pies: to seal a casserole or pie, or make a pie dish airtight, prepare some pastry by mixing 7 oz/200 g of flour with a glass of water. Roll out the pastry into a long, narrow sausage strip and place around the edge of the casserole lid to seal it. The contents will then be cooked by steaming, and the ingredients will retain all their flavour.

Fritters: make a very light batter for frying fritters, whether it's for coating fruits such as apples, pineapples or strawberries, acacia flowers, vegetables like salsify or Jerusalem artichokes, or the leaves of sorrel, parsley and sage. To prepare, mix 3½ oz/100 g of flour and a pinch of salt with a little water to produce a thick creamy consistency. Then add a tablespoon of oil and an equal amount of rum and leave to stand. When you're ready to use the batter, fold in one or two beaten egg whites, which will give it that extra smoothness and light frothiness.
- To make it easy to coat the pieces, stab the fruits, flowers, vegetables or leaves with a toothpick and then simply dip them into the batter.

Light, light, crêpes

Your crêpe batter will be much lighter if you add half a glass of beer or a whisked egg white to the milk.

French toast

Use stale bread or leftover brioche to make this delicious pudding, with its memories of childhood.

Serves 4:
- 4 slices stale bread
- 18 fl oz/½ l milk
- 1 egg, beaten
- 4 tablespoons oil
- 3½ oz/100 g butter
- 4 tablespoons caster sugar

Remove the crusts from the slices of bread and soak them in milk. Dip in the beaten egg, and sauté in a mixture of oil and butter, in a frying pan. Lift out the slices with a slice and remove the excess fat with kitchen paper. Sprinkle with sugar and serve.

CRÊPES AND PANCAKES: leave the batter to stand for at least an hour in the refrigerator (or better still, overnight); the crêpes will be much smoother.

■ For a more intense flavour, season the crêpe mixture just before use.

■ Grease a frying pan with a quarter of an apple, held on the prongs of a fork and dipped in oil, or use a knob of butter wrapped in muslin.

■ To reheat crêpes, pile on a plate, and place on top of a pan of hot water and cover with aluminium foil.

■ Revive any leftover crêpes by sprinkling with a mixture of warm rum and orange juice.

CAKES: should be cooked in a low oven (325°F/170°C/gas mark 3) and sometimes at an even lower heat if it is a particularly thick fruitcake, so that it cooks right through the middle.

■ Once you've placed your cake in the oven, make sure that you keep the oven door firmly closed for at least 15 minutes, to prevent the cake mixture from sinking.

■ For more even cooking, bake your cakes on a baking tray rather than directly on the oven shelf.

■ If the cake crust begins to brown too quickly or looks too dark for your liking, cover with a piece of greaseproof paper, before continuing to bake.

■ If the oven thermostat is faulty, a sheet of white paper, slipped into the oven, will give you an indication of the temperature: if it singes, the temperature is medium, if it blackens, the temperature is high.

■ To turn a cake out of a baking tin successfully, line the bottom of the cake tin with a piece of greaseproof paper, before pouring the mixture into the cake tin. You can also place the cake tin on a damp cloth for a few minutes, once the cake is cooked. Whichever method you use, grease the cake tin carefully and sprinkle with flour using a sieve or a tea strainer so the cake mix will spread more evenly in the tin.

■ Place cakes on a cake rack, after baking, to allow the steam to escape, this improves the cake's crumbly texture.

■ Create a chimney hole in fruitcake, midway through baking, so that the cake can rise.

■ Bake cakes in batches and freeze them. They'll come in handy for serving surprise guests.

■ A level teaspoon of bicarbonate of soda added to pain d'épice (spice bread) dough helps it rise. To enhance the flavour add some cloves.

Salt in cakes

Don't worry about using slightly salted butter for baking cakes – they'll be the tastier for it.

Pastry wheels

These useful kitchen gadgets not only make light work of trimming pastry for tarts and tartlets to any shape you could wish for, they can also add patterns to shortbread!

CRÈME ANGLAISE: this custard is much tastier when made with full-fat milk.

■ When making a creamy custard, split the vanilla pod lengthwise and open wide, in order to draw out the full vanilla fragrance.

■ When preparing *oeufs à la neige* poach the whipped egg whites of these snowy egg meringues in boiling water rather than in milk, which tends to darken the egg whites. Serve with custard.

Perfect rice pudding

When making rice pudding, add the sugar five minutes before the pudding has finished cooking, otherwise, it will affect the rice-cooking process. Sprinkle rice pudding with ground cinnamon before serving.

WHIPPED OR CHANTILLY CREAM: is more successful if all the ingredients as well as the mixer bowl are chilled, first.

■ Sweeten chantilly cream with icing sugar and flavour with ground ginger, immediately before serving.

CRÈME PATISSIÈRE OR CONFECTIONER'S CREAM: will be richer if you fold in 3¼ fl oz/10 cl of whipped crème fraîche. A tip is to add a small drop of pastis to this type of cream for added effect.

CUSTARD POTS: if the surface has cracked it has been over-cooked. To prevent this from happening, line the bottom of the base of the bain-marie with newspaper, before cooking.

RICE PUDDING: is made with short grain rice, blanched beforehand in cold, salted water and only then brought to the boil, to prevent the grains from splitting. Drain the rice and transfer immediately to the pan containing the boiling milk, flavoured with lemon zest, and then cook over a gentle heat for between 45 minutes and 1 hour.

ICE CREAM: if you're serving ice cream for pudding, don't forget to take it out of the freezer 15 minutes before eating. This allows the ice cream to regain its full flavour and it will also be smoother to the taste.

STEWED FRUIT: enhance the flavour of your compote by adding two tablespoons of an alcohol appropriate to the fruit used – calvados for stewed apples, plum brandy for stewed plums, kirsch for stewed cherries, and so on.

Semolina pudding

This is an easy pudding to make and it can be eaten hot or cold accompanied by stewed apple or a dollop of jam.

Serves 6:
■ 1¾ pt/1 l full-fat milk
■ 6 heaped teaspoons durum wheat semolina
■ 1 tablespoon rum
■ 4 tablespoons caster sugar
■ caramel

Boil the milk, then gradually drizzle the semolina into the milk, stirring continuously with a wooden spoon for five minutes. Add the sugar a minute before the pudding has finished cooking. Remove from the heat and add the rum. Serve in an attractive bowl and top with caramel.

BEVERAGES, ALCOHOL & INFUSIONS

TODAY DRINKS SUCH AS LIME-BLOSSOM AND VERBENA-FLAVOURED TEA, AND INFUSIONS MADE FROM GARDEN HERBS ARE ENJOYED FOR THEIR DIGESTIVE AND HEALTH-GIVING PROPERTIES. WE ARE REDISCOVERING THE PLEASURE OF ROUNDING OFF OUR MEALS WITH A TOUCH OF GENTILITY, BY OFFERING INFUSIONS AND OTHER LIQUID CONCOCTIONS. WE ARE ALSO RE-ACQUIRING THE TASTE FOR MAKING OUR OWN HOT CHOCOLATE, LEMONADE, APERITIFS AND AFTER-DINNER LIQUEURS. ALL THESE MAKE DELICIOUS DRINKS TO ENJOY IN THE COMPANY OF OUR FRIENDS.

HOT BEVERAGES

Hot chocolate

Here is a recipe for truly rich and frothy hot chocolate. This delicious beverage should be drunk hot, but not boiling.

Makes 4 cups:
- 1¾ pt/1 l full-fat milk
- 3 oz/80 g dark, bitter cocoa powder (of the Van Houten variety)
- 4 tablespoons caster sugar

Bring the milk to the boil. Mix the cocoa powder with some of the milk and return to the boiling milk. Cook for three minutes, over a gentle heat, stirring continuously. If you're not keen on the skin off the milk, sieve the hot chocolate through a small conical strainer before serving.

COFFEE: keeps best in the refrigerator, or even the freezer, for several months. Store in a hermetically sealed container.
- To intensify the aroma of your coffee, add two grains of salt to the ground coffee in your coffee filter.
- Add three drops of cold water to boiled coffee to eliminate the bitter taste.
- If your fingers smell of garlic or onion, rub with coffee grounds.
- Remove a coffee stain from fabric by rubbing in a solution of hydrogen peroxide or vinegar and water.
- Don't stir Irish coffee once you've poured in the cream, because its highly coveted aroma is delivered as the hot coffee and whisky is sipped through the cream topping.
- Add 3 or 4 tablespoons of chocolate ice cream to iced coffee, to get a combined dessert and thirst-quenching summer drink.

TEA: Add the hot water to your teapot, just when it reaches boiling point to make your tea taste better.
- Enhance ordinary tea by adding small pieces of broken vanilla pod or grated ginger when preparing an infusion.
- To draw the flavour out of tea, place a piece of dried orange peel in your tea caddy.
- Pour tea into cold milk, and not the other way round. Cold milk combines more easily with the tannins in tea.
- For a quick and easy recipe for iced tea, just add a few ice cubes to strong, hot, infused tea.
- Green tea is a relaxing tea to drink in the afternoon. You can also use green tea as a substitute for the syrup in a fresh fruit salad. To prepare, infuse some mint leaves and oregano, a cinnamon stick and a vanilla pod in green tea; add 2 tablespoons of unrefined sugar; leave to chill and pour over the fruit salad.

Even better than cappuccino

What could be better than a cappuccino? A cappuccino flavoured with the grated zest of an orange and sprinkle generously with chocolate powder.

CHOCOLATE: flavour your hot chocolate in a variety of different ways: add a dash of strong coffee or rum immediately before serving, or infuse the milk with a vanilla pod halved lengthwise or a cinnamon stick.

ALCOHOLIC DRINKS

WINE: do not use corked wines for making sauces because the corked taste will be overpowering and more than likely will ruin the sauce.

- Use leftover white or red wine in fresh fruit salads or with dried fruit in syrup desserts. Simply reduce the wine over heat and store in a preserving jar in the refrigerator. It is then readily available for preparing sauces.
- If you don't have any white wine to hand for making a sauce, mix 3½ fl oz/10 cl of white wine vinegar with an equal volume of water, and add two lumps of sugar. This yields the equivalent of a glass of white wine.
- If wine is not at the correct room temperature, don't put the bottle itself in warm water, instead place the carafe into which the wine is to be decanted directly into the warm water.
- Make orange wine to serve with aperitifs or as an after dinner liqueur. Macerate the zest of two un-waxed oranges (peeled using a paring knife), in 3½ pt/2 litres of white wine and 1 fl oz/25 cl of brandy or another 45° proof spirit to which 1lb 2oz/500 g of sugar has been added. Filter after three weeks and store, corked, for several months before drinking.
- Cleaning a carafe encrusted with calcium deposits is easy; simply pour a handful of cooking salt and a tablespoon of vinegar into the carafe, seal and shake vigorously.

SPIRITS: offer guests a glass of chilled white armagnac to accompany part-cooked foie gras or smoked fish. If it is served mid-way through a lavish meal, this drink aids digestion.

- Recommend a flaming plum- or pear-brandy to your guests to round off a memorable meal. To prepare, flambé the spirit with sugar – it is a sociable gesture, and also reduces its alcohol content.
- Offer guests a glass of calvados to accompany iced apple sorbet for dessert, or as a drink to enjoy between the courses of an elaborate meal.

Rose *kir royale*

To make rose *kir royale*, add a tablespoon of rose water to a glass of blackcurrant liqueur and champagne, and for that finishing touch, decorate each glass with a rose petal. You could adapt the recipe by using blueberry, redcurrant, blackberry or strawberry juice to make variations on *kir royale*.

Frosted glasses

To frost the rim of a glass, moisten the rim with lemon juice and dip in caster sugar.

Homemade lemonade

Make your own real lemonade and give it a festive twist by adding a handful of redcurrants to each glass.

Makes 1¾ pt/1 litre of lemonade:

- 18 fl oz/50 cl still water
- 6 tablespoons caster sugar
- 5 unwaxed lemons
- 18 fl oz/50 cl fizzy water
- 1 tablespoon grenadine
- 3½ oz/100 g redcurrants

Boil the still water with the sugar and 1 lemon cut into rounds with the rind left on. Add the juice and flesh of the remaining lemons. Mix all the ingredients in a blender, strain through a filter and cool. Add the fizzy water and finally the grenadine, garnish with a few redcurrants. Serve very chilled.

CHAMPAGNE: to quick-chill a bottle of champagne, add a handful of rock salt to the ice bucket.

- Use champagne dregs instead of wine or water to cook dried fruit.

NON-ALCOHOLIC COCKTAILS: to create quick and easy, non-alcoholic cocktails mix a spoonful of squash or cordial with fruit juices: mix 1 tablespoon of strawberry cordial or squash in a glass of pineapple juice; 1 tablespoon of raspberry cordial in a glass of grapefruit juice; 1 tablespoon of grenadine cordial in a glass of orange juice.

- Make non-alcoholic sangria, by replacing the wine with red grape juice. Immediately before serving, add 1¾ pt/1 l of chilled lemonade to every 3½ pt/2 l of grape juice.

CHILLED DRINKS AND INFUSIONS

WATER: if you don't have a picnic cooler bag for your water, keep it cool by wrapping the bottle in several layers of newspaper or a chilled, damp tea towel and leave in the shade.

- Rub sugar lumps over lemon or orange peel and use to add fragrance to fresh chilled water.
- Add lime-flavoured ice cubes to fresh water: pour a little lime cordial into each ice cube compartment, top up with water and leave in the freezer for at least two hours.

INFUSIONS: at the end of each season, dry the leaves and flowers of verbena, sage, rosemary, thyme, cherry stalks, rosebuds, citronella, and apple slices or apple skins. Store the dried plants in a hermetically sealed decorative jar and use the mixture to make original herbal teas.

- After dinner, offer a convivial and tasty concoction of fruits and herbs to make a herbal tea. In summer, add a choice of soft fruits, peaches, nectarines, a sprig of thyme, rosemary, or verbena to boiling water. Boil for 10 minutes, then strain and pour into an attractive heat resistant carafe; garnish with some fresh soft fruits. In autumn, use unpeeled pears, figs, and grapes; in winter try apples and kiwis, adding a piece of star anise, cinnamon, and a pinch of dried flowers and leaves.

Iced infusions

Prepare an infusion using mint or verbena; leave to chill in the refrigerator for 2 hours. Serve iced with a slice of lemon, a mint or verbena leaf and some ice cubes.

SUPPLEMENTS

INDEX

Alcohol, 128, 151, 152

Anchovies, salted, 67

Anise, 32

Apples, 117, 118

Apricots, 114

Apricots, dried, 128

Artichokes, 52

Asparagus, 42

Aubergines, 56

Avocados, 56

Bananas, 114

Basil, 22

Bay, 25, 26

Beans, dried, 60

Beans, French, 52

Béchamel, 10, 13, 14

Beef, 81

Beetroot, 52

Beverages, hot, 148

Black pudding, 82

Bouquet garni, 26

Bread, 132, 135

Breadcrumbs, 78

Bulgar wheat, 110

Butter, 96

Cabbage, 49

Cakes, 136, 141

Capers, 36

Caramel, 141

Cardamom, 35

Carrots, 45, 46

Cauliflower, 49

Celeriac, 46

Cereals, 110

Champagne, 152

Cheese, 99

Cherries, 118

Chestnuts, 128

Chicken, 89

Chickpeas, 60

Chicory, 45

Chives, 22

Chocolate, 141, 142, 148, 151

Citrus fruit, 122, 125, 126

Clams, 74

Cloves, 32

Cockles, 74

Cocktails, non-alcoholic, 152

Cod, 68

Coffee, 148

Compote, 145

Condiments, 36, 39

Coriander, 22

Courgette, 42, 45

Crab, 73

Crayfish, saltwater, 73

Crème Anglaise (custard), 142, 145

Chantilly cream, 142, 145

Crème Patissière, 145

Crêpes, 135

Crystallised fruits, 126, 128

Cucumber, 56

Cumin, 32

Curry, 32, 35

Custard Pots, 145

Dairy products, 96, 99

Desserts, 142, 145

Dressings, 17, 18

Drinks, chilled, 152

Duck, 86

Egg liaison, 14

Eggs, 92, 95, 96

Eggs, fried, 95

Eggs, hard-boiled, 92

Eggs, poached, 95

Eggs, scrambled, 95

Eggs, soft-boiled, 95

Figs, 114

Fish, 64, 67, 68

Five-spice, 35

Flour, 132

Foie gras, 86

Fritters, 135

Fromage blanc, 99

Fruit, dried, 126, 128

Fruit, fresh, 114, 117, 118, 122–126

Fruits, preserved, 126, 128

Fruits, soft, 118, 122

Game, 86, 89

Garlic, 26, 31

Gherkins, 36

Ginger, 39

Grapefruit, 125

Grapes, 118

Guinea fowl, 89

Hare, 89

Hazelnuts, 128

Herbs, 22, 25, 26

Honey, 132, 142

Horseradish, 52

Hyssop, 25

Ice cream, 145

Infusions, 152

Jams, 126

Jelly, 126

Kumquats, 125

Lamb, 78, 81

Leeks, 46

Lemon, 122, 125

Lentils, 60

Liquorice, 35

Lobster, 73
Mace, 32
Mackerel, 64, 67
Mangoes, 117
Marinades, 18
Marinade, spice-based, 18
Marinade, yoghurt-based, 18
Mayonnaise, 13
Mayonnaise, garlic, 13
Meat, 78, 81, 82, 86
Melon, 117
Milk, 96, 99
Mint, 22
Mushrooms, 59
Mushrooms, button, 59
Mushrooms, cep, 59
Mussels, 74
Mustard, 39
Nutmeg, 32
Nuts, 128
Octopus, 73
Oil, vegetable, 17
Olives, 39
Omelette, 95, 96
Onion, 26, 31
Oranges, 125
Oysters, 73, 74
Pancakes and crêpes, 135, 136
Parsley, 22, 25
Pasta sauces, 105, 109
Pasta, 102, 105, 109
Pasta, dried, 105
Pasta, fresh, 105
Pastry for sealing pies, 135
Pastry, puff, 135
Pastry, shortcrust, 135
Pastry, tart, 132

Pâtisserie, 132, 135, 136, 141, 142
Peaches, 114
Pears, 117,
Peas, 52
Peas, split, 60
Pepper, 35, 36
Pepper, Espelette, 35
Peppers, 56
Pineapple, 114
Pork, 82
Potatoes, 46, 49
Poultry, 86, 89
Prawns, 73
Prunes, 128
Pumpkin, 49
Quail, 89
Quinces, 117, 118
Quinoa, 110
Rabbit, 89
Radishes, 56
Raspberries, 122
Red mullet, 68
Redcurrants, 122, 126
Rice pudding, 145
Rice, 109, 110
Rosemary, 25, 26
Saffron, 35
Sage, 25
Salad, 55
Salmon, 18, 68
Salt, 36
Sardines, 67
Sauce, tomato, 14
Sauces, wine-based, 14
Sauces, 10, 13, 14, 17
Scallops, 68, 74
Sea urchins, 74

Seafood, 73, 74
Seasonings, 26, 31
Semolina, 110, 145
Shellfish, 73, 74
Shrimps, 73
Sole, 68
Spelt, 110
Spices, 31, 32, 35, 36
Spinach, 58
Spirits, 151
Squid, 68
Star anise, 32
Strawberries, 118, 122
Sugar, 32, 142
Tarragon, 22
Tea, 148
Thyme, 25, 26
Tomatoes, 55, 110
Truffles, 59, 92
Tuna, 68
Vanilla, 31, 32
Veal, 82
Vegetables, dried, 60
Vegetables, fresh, 42, 45, 46, 49, 52,
  55, 56, 59
Verbena, 25, 26
Vinaigrette, 17
Vinegar, 17, 18
Water, 152
Whelks, 73
Wine, 151
Yoghurt, 99

INDEX OF RECIPES

Beetroot purée 52

Coddled quails eggs 92

Classic mayonnaise 13

Eggs mimosa 95

French toast 135

Fresh egg pasta 105

Homemade lemonade 152

Hot chocolate 148

Mango chutney 117

Marinated salmon fillets 18

Milanese risotto 109

Mona dressing 17

Pesto 22

Potted mackerel 64

Preserved lemons 125

Pumpkin gratin 49

Ravigote sauce 14

Salted foie gras 86

Semolina pudding 145

Small flavoured custards 141

Split pea purée 60

Steamed shoulder of lamb 81

Strawberry soup 122

Tapenade 39

Vegetarian stuffed tomatoes 110

Walnut wine 128

EQUIVALENT MEASUREMENTS

Weighing without scales:

- 1 level tablespoonful equals:
  20 g rice
  20 g flour
  20 g caster sugar
  25 g cooking salt
  20 g water.

- 1 mustard jar holds 20 cl of liquid.

- 1 liqueur glass holds 2 to 3 cl of liquid.

- 1 egg weighs 60 to 80 g.

- A yoghurt pot can be used to measure:
  125 g liquid
  125 g sugar
  125 g rice
  85 g flour.

Oven temperature conversion chart:

110°C (225°F)	=	Gas Mark ¼
130°C (250°F)	=	Gas Mark ½
140°C (275°F)	=	Gas Mark 1
150°C (300°F)	=	Gas Mark 2
170°C (325°F)	=	Gas Mark 3
180°C (350°F)	=	Gas Mark 4
190°C (375°F)	=	Gas Mark 5
200°C (400°F)	=	Gas Mark 6
220°C (425°F)	=	Gas Mark 7
230°C (450°F)	=	Gas Mark 8
240°C (475°F)	=	Gas Mark 9

STORE CUPBOARD, REFRIGERATOR OR FREEZER ESSENTIALS

SAVE TIME AND ENERGY BY HAVING THESE ESSENTIAL INGREDIENTS TO HAND; THIS WILL ENABLE YOU TO COOK QUICKLY, EFFECTIVELY, EVEN AT SHORT NOTICE.

Store cupboard or refrigerator ingredients:

■ Bicarbonate of soda, useful for cooking dried vegetables, removing acidity from tomatoes and as a substitute for yeast in recipes. A mere pinch of bicarbonate of soda mixed in water aids digestion.

■ Onion essence or stock cubes for colouring bouillons, stock or wine-based sauces.

■ Poultry or vegetable stock concentrates for thickening or improving soups.

■ Espelette pepper for flavouring and seasoning, and for replacing pepper in recipes.

■ A variety of different peppercorns (Szechwan, black pepper, white Cameroon pepper, etc).

■ Unrefined natural sea salt, for its far superior flavour compared with refined salt..

■ Fresh spices (saffron, curry, cumin, nutmeg, cloves).

■ Natural *Agen* prunes for enhancing sauces and improvised desserts.

■ Dark chocolate for colouring sauces and stews.

■ Seasoned dried breadcrumbs for use in gratin dishes or for mixing with flour for making cakes.

■ Different flavoured olive oils and vinegars for a variety of salad dressings.

■ Shallots, garlic and onions are indispensable for basic, everyday cooking.

■ Potatoes (ah! those wonderful chips, on Sunday evenings, when there are no other vegetables left).

■ Tinned anchovies and sardines for making sauces, accompanying crudités or to serve with aperitifs.

■ Cans of tomato purée for a make-shift sauce, or as a substitute for winter tomatoes that often leave much to be desired.

■ Preserved red peppers for making pasta sauces.

■ Vanilla pods and cinnamon sticks for making spur-of-the-moment puddings.

■ Different types of rice for making risottos, puddings, and curries; and pasta, always a handy ingredient for a quick meal.

■ A heel of ham for cooking, and the remains for flavouring cabbage soup.

■ Some shoulder of salted pork.

■ Block of parmesan, always useful for salads, carpaccio, pasta and rice dishes.

Freezer ingredients:

■ Aromatic herbs for flavouring soups and gratin dishes.

■ Flavoured ice cubes for pepping up last-minute dishes.

■ Homemade tomato sauce, to pop in the frying pan as an accompaniment for pasta or eggs.

■ Meat stock for cooking risotto.

■ A fresh truffle for a bit of extra flair, or for adding a festive touch to pasta recipes.

■ Pastry for making sweet or savoury tarts.

ACKNOWLEDGEMENTS

My mother, who bestowed upon me a love of cooking.

José and Pierre, for their invaluable artistic and culinary advice.

Henry and Françoise Quinta, for their fine kitchen.

Françoise Lefébure and Gérard Vives, for their support.

Résonances, Mathias, Kim&Garo, for the crockery.

Maison Fassier, for the linen.

Claudine Picart, for her quince display.

Dani and Carla Bruni, for background music.

Valérie, for her tolerance and support throughout our project.

And all our friends who readily divulged their kitchen secrets!

Editorial: Valérie Tognali
Artwork: Nancy Dorking
Graphic Design: Gaëlle Chartier
Page-setting: Irène de Moucheron
Proofreading: Chloé Chauveau
Production: Nicole Thiériot-Pichon
Photoengraving: Reproscan

First published by Editions du Chêne,
an imprint of Hachette-Livre
43 Quai de Grenelle, Paris 75905, Cedex 15, France
Under the title *Secrets du cuisine*
© 2004, Editions du Chêne / Hachette-Livre
All rights reserved

English language translation produced by Translate-A-Book, Oxford

This edition published by Hachette Illustrated UK, Octopus Publishing Group,
2–4 Heron Quays, London, E14 4JP
English Translation © 2005, Octopus Publishing Group Ltd, London

ISBN 10: 1 84430 149 4
ISBN 13: 978 1 84430 149 2
Printed by Toppan Printing Co., (HK) Ltd.